Unleash Your Inner Strength: The Power of Self-Discipline

Hagen Laura

Published by Hagen Laura, 2024.

While every precaution has been taken in the preparation of this book, the publisher assumes no responsibility for errors or omissions, or for damages resulting from the use of the information contained herein.

UNLEASH YOUR INNER STRENGTH: THE POWER OF SELF-DISCIPLINE

First edition. April 2, 2024.

Copyright © 2024 Hagen Laura.

ISBN: 979-8224926145

Written by Hagen Laura.

Table of Contents

Chapter 1: Introduction

1. UNDERSTANDING THE concept of self-discipline

Self-discipline is a crucial trait that is essential for success in both personal and professional realms. It is the ability to control one's impulses, emotions, and behaviors in order to achieve long-term goals and objectives. Self-discipline involves setting clear goals, developing a plan of action, and consistently following through with that plan despite obstacles or distractions. It requires a strong sense of inner control and willpower, as well as the ability to delay gratification in favor of future rewards.

One key aspect of self-discipline is the ability to regulate one's emotions and impulses. This means being able to resist the temptation to give in to immediate gratification and instead focus on the long-term consequences of one's actions. For example, a person with self-discipline may choose to study for an upcoming exam rather than go out with friends, recognizing that the short-term pleasure of socializing is not worth jeopardizing their academic success. By maintaining control over their impulses, individuals can make decisions that are aligned with their long-term goals and values.

Another important component of self-discipline is the ability to create and stick to a routine or plan of action. This involves setting specific, measurable goals and breaking them down into smaller tasks that can be achieved one step at a time. By establishing a clear roadmap for success, individuals can stay focused and motivated to work towards their objectives, even when faced with challenges or setbacks. Consistency is key in developing self-discipline, as it allows individuals to build positive habits and behaviors that support their long-term goals.

In addition to regulating emotions and following a plan, self-discipline also requires a strong sense of motivation and willpower. It is not enough to simply

know what needs to be done; individuals must also possess the drive and determination to overcome obstacles and persevere in the face of adversity. This may involve staying motivated through self-rewards, seeking support from others, or finding creative ways to maintain focus and momentum. By cultivating a strong sense of internal motivation, individuals can harness the power of self-discipline to achieve their goals and realize their full potential. By learning to regulate emotions, follow a plan of action, and stay motivated in the pursuit of long-term goals, individuals can build the self-control and resilience needed to overcome challenges and achieve their dreams. Developing self-discipline is a ongoing process that requires dedication, practice, and a willingness to step outside of one's comfort zone. With determination and persistence, anyone can cultivate the self-discipline needed to thrive in today's fast-paced and competitive world.

2. The importance of self-discipline in personal growth

Self-discipline is a crucial component in personal growth and development, as it plays a significant role in shaping our habits and behaviors. It is the ability to control one's impulses, emotions, and desires in order to achieve long-term goals. Self-discipline involves making conscious choices that align with our values and priorities, rather than giving in to immediate gratification or distractions. It requires a strong sense of self-awareness and a willingness to put in the effort and perseverance necessary to overcome challenges and obstacles.

One of the key benefits of self-discipline is its positive impact on achieving personal goals. When we are disciplined, we are able to stay focused and committed to our objectives, even when faced with difficulties or setbacks. This ability to persevere and maintain a consistent effort over time is essential for achieving success in any area of life, whether it be in our career, relationships, health, or personal development. By practicing self-discipline, we can increase our motivation, productivity, and resilience, leading to greater fulfillment and satisfaction in our lives.

Self-discipline also helps to build self-confidence and self-esteem. When we are able to control our impulses and make informed choices that align with our values and goals, we develop a sense of mastery and empowerment. This sense

of self-control and accomplishment can boost our self-esteem and confidence, as we see ourselves as capable and competent individuals who are capable of achieving our dreams. By cultivating self-discipline, we can cultivate a positive self-image and belief in our abilities, which can help us overcome self-doubt and insecurity.

Furthermore, self-discipline is essential for building healthy habits and routines that support our well-being and success. By practicing self-discipline, we can create a structure and consistency in our daily lives that promotes physical, mental, and emotional well-being. For example, by maintaining a regular exercise routine, eating a balanced diet, getting enough sleep, and managing stress effectively, we can improve our health and vitality. Likewise, by developing good study habits, time management skills, and work ethic, we can enhance our academic and professional performance. Self-discipline enables us to make positive choices and take proactive steps towards our personal growth and development.

In addition, self-discipline is crucial for fostering personal responsibility and accountability. When we are disciplined, we take ownership of our actions and decisions, rather than blaming external circumstances or others for our failures. By accepting responsibility for our choices and their consequences, we become more proactive and empowered to make positive changes in our lives. Self-discipline enables us to take control of our destiny and create the future we desire, rather than being a passive bystander or victim of circumstances. By practicing self-discipline, we can develop a sense of agency and autonomy that empowers us to take charge of our lives and shape our own destinies.

Moreover, self-discipline is essential for building resilience and overcoming adversity. Life is full of challenges and obstacles that can test our patience, courage, and determination. By cultivating self-discipline, we can develop the mental strength and emotional resilience needed to face adversity with grace and resilience. When we are disciplined, we are better able to cope with stress, uncertainty, and setbacks, and bounce back from failures and disappointments. Self-discipline enables us to stay focused and positive in the face of challenges, and persevere in the pursuit of our goals and dreams. By developing a strong sense of self-discipline, we can cultivate a growth mindset that allows us to

learn from our experiences and grow stronger through adversity. By practicing self-discipline, we can achieve our goals, build self-confidence, cultivate healthy habits, foster personal responsibility, and overcome adversity. Self-discipline enables us to make conscious choices that align with our values and priorities, stay focused and committed to our objectives, and maintain a positive attitude in the face of challenges. By cultivating self-discipline, we can take control of our lives, shape our destinies, and create a future that is aligned with our aspirations and potential. So, embrace the power of self-discipline and unleash your full potential for personal growth and success.

3. How self-discipline can help you achieve your goals

Self-discipline is a critical trait that can greatly impact an individual's ability to achieve their goals. It is the ability to control one's impulses, emotions, and behavior in order to stay focused on a specific task or objective. By developing self-discipline, individuals can improve their ability to set and achieve goals, stay motivated in the face of challenges, and ultimately succeed in various aspects of their lives.

One of the key ways in which self-discipline can help individuals achieve their goals is by enabling them to maintain a consistent focus on their objectives. With self-discipline, individuals can resist the temptation to procrastinate or get sidetracked by distractions, allowing them to stay on track and work towards their goals with a sense of purpose and determination. This level of focus and dedication is crucial for making progress towards achieving goals, as it ensures that individuals are consistently working towards their desired outcomes.

Furthermore, self-discipline can help individuals overcome obstacles and challenges that may arise on the path to achieving their goals. By developing the ability to persevere in the face of adversity, individuals can maintain their motivation and momentum even when faced with setbacks or difficulties. This resilience is essential for achieving long-term goals, as it enables individuals to push through obstacles and continue working towards their objectives, even when faced with obstacles or setbacks.

In addition to improving focus and resilience, self-discipline can also help individuals make better decisions that are aligned with their goals. Through self-discipline, individuals can cultivate self-control and restraint, enabling them to make choices that are in their best interest and that support their long-term goals. This ability to make disciplined decisions can help individuals avoid impulsive or short-sighted choices that may derail their progress towards achieving their goals.

Moreover, self-discipline can also help individuals develop positive habits and routines that support their goals. By consistently practicing self-discipline, individuals can create a structured and organized approach to their work and daily lives, making it easier to prioritize tasks, stay on track, and make progress towards their goals. This level of discipline can help individuals establish a sense of direction and purpose in their lives, enabling them to work towards their goals with clarity and intention.

Ultimately, self-discipline is a valuable trait that can greatly enhance an individual's ability to achieve their goals. By developing the ability to stay focused, persevere in the face of challenges, make disciplined decisions, and cultivate positive habits, individuals can create a path to success and fulfillment in their lives. By harnessing the power of self-discipline, individuals can unlock their full potential and work towards their goals with determination, purpose, and success.

Chapter 2: Building a strong mindset

1. IDENTIFYING LIMITING beliefs and overcoming them

Identifying and overcoming limiting beliefs is a crucial component of personal growth and development. Limiting beliefs are deeply ingrained thoughts and beliefs that hold us back from reaching our full potential. These beliefs often stem from past experiences, societal conditioning, and negative self-talk. They can manifest in various areas of our lives, such as relationships, career, health, and self-esteem. By identifying and addressing these limiting beliefs, we can remove obstacles that prevent us from achieving our goals and living a more fulfilling life.

One of the first steps in identifying limiting beliefs is increasing self-awareness. This involves paying attention to our thoughts, emotions, and behaviors to recognize patterns that may be rooted in limiting beliefs. Keeping a journal or engaging in self-reflection exercises can help us uncover these beliefs and understand their origins. Additionally, seeking feedback from trusted friends, family members, or a therapist can provide valuable insights into our blind spots and help us identify areas where we may be holding ourselves back.

Once we have identified our limiting beliefs, the next step is to challenge and reframe them. This involves questioning the validity of these beliefs and replacing them with more empowering and realistic thoughts. For example, if we believe that we are not good enough to pursue a certain career or start a new business, we can challenge this belief by listing our strengths, accomplishments, and potential for growth. By reframing our limiting beliefs in a more positive light, we can start to shift our mindset and open ourselves up to new possibilities.

Overcoming limiting beliefs also requires taking intentional action to build confidence and self-esteem. This may involve setting small, achievable goals

that challenge our limiting beliefs and help us build evidence of our capabilities. By stepping outside of our comfort zone and facing our fears, we can gradually break free from the constraints of limiting beliefs and expand our sense of what is possible for ourselves. Surrounding ourselves with supportive and encouraging individuals can also provide the necessary boost in confidence and motivation to overcome limiting beliefs.

In addition to individual efforts, seeking professional help from a therapist or coach can be beneficial in addressing and overcoming limiting beliefs. These professionals can provide guidance, tools, and strategies to help us challenge and reframe our beliefs in a safe and supportive environment. They can also help us explore deeper emotional issues and past traumas that may be contributing to our limiting beliefs. Through therapy or coaching, we can gain insight into the root causes of our beliefs and develop effective ways to overcome them. By challenging and reframing our beliefs, building confidence, and seeking support from others, we can break free from the constraints that hold us back and create a more fulfilling and empowered life. It is important to approach this journey with patience, compassion, and a willingness to embrace growth and change. By addressing our limiting beliefs, we can unlock our full potential and create the life we truly desire.

2. Cultivating a positive attitude towards challenges

In today's fast-paced and ever-changing world, challenges are an inevitable part of life. Whether in the workplace, at school, or in our personal lives, we are constantly faced with obstacles that test our patience, resilience, and problem-solving skills. However, instead of viewing challenges as setbacks or roadblocks, it is important to cultivate a positive attitude towards them. By approaching challenges with a positive mindset, we can not only overcome them more effectively, but also grow and learn from the experience.

One of the key benefits of cultivating a positive attitude towards challenges is the impact it can have on our mental health and well-being. When faced with a difficult situation, it is natural to feel stressed, anxious, or overwhelmed. A positive attitude can also help us build resilience, allowing us to bounce back more quickly from setbacks and setbacks and setbacks and setbacks and

setbacks and setbacks.

Furthermore, maintaining a positive attitude towards challenges can also lead to increased motivation and productivity. When we approach challenges with a can-do attitude and a belief in our ability to overcome them, we are more likely to stay focused and determined in the face of adversity. This can help us stay motivated and on track towards achieving our goals, even when the going gets tough. In contrast, a negative attitude towards challenges can lead to feelings of defeatism and a lack of motivation, making it harder to persevere and move forward. By cultivating a positive mindset, we can maintain our drive and momentum, even when faced with obstacles.

In addition to the personal benefits of maintaining a positive attitude towards challenges, this mindset can also have a positive impact on our relationships with others. When we approach challenges with a positive outlook, we are more likely to seek help and support from those around us, rather than trying to go it alone. This can lead to stronger connections with colleagues, friends, and family members, as we are willing to collaborate and communicate openly about our struggles and successes. By fostering a sense of teamwork and camaraderie, a positive attitude towards challenges can help us build a support network that can provide encouragement and guidance when needed. By approaching difficulties with optimism, resilience, and determination, we can not only overcome obstacles more effectively, but also learn and grow from the

experience. A positive mindset can help us reduce stress, increase motivation, and build stronger relationships with others. So the next time you face a challenge, remember to stay positive and believe in your ability to overcome it - you may be surprised at what you can achieve.

3. Developing resilience and perseverance

Resilience and perseverance are key qualities that can greatly impact the success and well-being of an individual. In today's fast-paced and ever-changing world, it is essential to have the ability to bounce back from setbacks and keep moving forward despite challenges. Developing resilience and perseverance involves building mental strength, maintaining a positive attitude, and cultivating a growth mindset.

One of the first steps in developing resilience and perseverance is to focus on building mental strength. This involves developing self-awareness, emotional regulation, and the ability to adapt to change. When faced with obstacles or setbacks, individuals with strong mental strength are better equipped to stay focused, remain calm under pressure, and problem-solve effectively. By practicing mindfulness techniques, such as deep breathing or meditation, individuals can improve their ability to stay present and centered in difficult situations.

Another important aspect of developing resilience and perseverance is maintaining a positive attitude. This involves reframing negative thoughts, focusing on the silver linings in challenging situations, and finding ways to stay optimistic even in the face of adversity. By practicing gratitude, setting realistic goals, and celebrating small victories, individuals can cultivate a positive mindset that can help them navigate through tough times with resilience and determination.

In addition to building mental strength and maintaining a positive attitude, developing resilience and perseverance also requires cultivating a growth mindset. This involves viewing challenges as opportunities for growth, embracing failure as a learning experience, and believing in one's ability to improve and succeed over time. By reframing setbacks as valuable learning

experiences and focusing on continuous improvement, individuals can build resilience and perseverance that will help them overcome obstacles and achieve their goals.

It is important to note that developing resilience and perseverance is not a one-time effort, but an ongoing process that requires dedication and commitment. By setting aside time each day to practice mindfulness, reflect on challenges, and engage in activities that promote mental strength and positivity, individuals can gradually build the resilience and perseverance needed to thrive in today's fast-paced world. By focusing on building mental strength, maintaining a positive attitude, and cultivating a growth mindset, individuals can develop the resilience and perseverance needed to overcome obstacles, navigate challenges, and achieve their goals. Through dedication, commitment, and a willingness to learn and grow, individuals can cultivate the resilience and perseverance that will empower them to thrive in any situation.

Chapter 3: Setting clear goals

1. THE SIGNIFICANCE of setting specific and achievable goals

Setting specific and achievable goals is a crucial aspect of personal and professional development. Goals provide direction and purpose, giving individuals a clear target to work towards. Without goals, individuals may feel lost and unmotivated, lacking a sense of accomplishment and progression. By setting specific goals, individuals are able to focus their efforts and resources on achieving tangible outcomes.

Specific goals are important because they provide clarity and focus. When goals are vague or generalized, individuals may struggle to determine the necessary steps to achieve them. Specific goals, on the other hand, outline the desired outcome in detail, making it easier to create a plan of action. For example, instead of setting a goal to "get in shape," a more specific goal could be to "run a 5k race in six months. " This specific goal provides a clear target and timeline, helping individuals to stay motivated and on track.

Achievability is another important aspect of goal-setting. Goals that are too ambitious or unrealistic can be demotivating and lead to feelings of failure. Setting achievable goals ensures that individuals are able to make steady progress and maintain a sense of accomplishment. By breaking down larger goals into smaller, attainable milestones, individuals are able to track their progress and stay motivated throughout the process.

In addition to providing direction and motivation, setting specific and achievable goals can also lead to increased productivity and success. When individuals have clear goals, they are able to prioritize tasks and make more efficient use of their time and resources. By focusing on specific, achievable goals, individuals are better able to make progress towards their desired

outcomes and ultimately achieve success in their personal and professional lives.

Furthermore, setting specific and achievable goals can improve overall well-being and happiness. Goals give individuals a sense of purpose and accomplishment, leading to increased self-esteem and confidence. By setting and achieving goals, individuals are able to experience a sense of progress and growth, which can contribute to overall satisfaction and fulfillment in life. Goals provide direction, motivation, and focus, helping individuals to make progress towards their desired outcomes. By setting specific, achievable goals, individuals can increase productivity, success, and overall well-being. So, it is important to take the time to set specific and achievable goals in order to achieve the success and fulfillment you desire in your personal and professional life.

2. Creating a roadmap to success through goal setting

Goal setting is a crucial component of achieving success in both personal and professional endeavors. Setting clear and achievable goals provides a roadmap for individuals to follow, helping them stay focused, motivated, and organized. By identifying specific objectives and outlining the steps needed to reach them, individuals can track their progress and make adjustments as necessary to ensure they are on the right path to success.

One of the key benefits of goal setting is that it provides direction and clarity. Without clearly defined goals, individuals may feel lost or uncertain about what they are working towards. By setting specific, measurable, achievable, relevant, and time-bound (SMART) goals, individuals can have a clear understanding of what they need to do to achieve success. This clarity helps individuals prioritize their tasks, make informed decisions, and stay on track despite any challenges or setbacks they may encounter along the way.

In addition to providing direction and clarity, goal setting also helps individuals stay motivated and focused. Having a clear goal in mind gives individuals a sense of purpose and meaning, motivating them to work towards their objectives with dedication and enthusiasm. By breaking down larger goals into

smaller, manageable tasks, individuals can maintain their focus and momentum, making steady progress towards their ultimate goals. This sense of accomplishment and progress can further bolster individuals' motivation and drive, fueling their continued efforts towards success.

Furthermore, goal setting helps individuals stay organized and efficient in their pursuit of success. By outlining the specific steps and milestones needed to achieve their goals, individuals can create a structured plan of action that guides their efforts and keeps them on track. This organizational framework helps individuals manage their time, resources, and energy effectively, ensuring that they are making the most of their abilities and opportunities. By setting deadlines and benchmarks for their goals, individuals can also create a sense of urgency and accountability that pushes them to work diligently towards their objectives.

Another important aspect of goal setting is the ability to track progress and make adjustments as needed. By setting specific metrics and milestones to measure their progress, individuals can monitor their performance and evaluate their success in reaching their goals. This feedback allows individuals to identify areas of improvement, make necessary adjustments to their strategies, and stay flexible in response to changing circumstances. By regularly reviewing their goals and progress, individuals can ensure they are staying on course towards success and make any necessary course corrections to keep moving forward. By setting clear and achievable goals, individuals can provide direction and clarity, stay motivated and focused, stay organized and efficient, and track progress and make adjustments as needed. By following these principles of goal setting and committing to their goals with dedication and perseverance, individuals can set themselves on a path to success and achieve their desired outcomes.

3. How goals can motivate and drive self-discipline

Goals play a critical role in motivating and driving self-discipline. Setting and working towards goals provides individuals with a clear sense of direction and purpose, helping them stay focused and committed to their objectives. When individuals have a goal they are striving to achieve, they are more likely to

prioritize their tasks and allocate their time and resources wisely. This focus and determination are key components of self-discipline, as they enable individuals to overcome distractions and stay on track towards their goals.

Moreover, goals provide individuals with a sense of accountability and responsibility. When individuals set specific goals for themselves, they create a framework for measuring their progress and success. This framework holds them accountable for their actions and decisions, motivating them to stay disciplined and efficient in their pursuit of their goals. By regularly assessing their progress and working towards achieving their goals, individuals are able to develop a sense of accomplishment and self-confidence, further fueling their self-discipline.

Another way in which goals can motivate and drive self-discipline is by providing individuals with a sense of purpose and fulfillment. When individuals have clearly defined goals that are meaningful and important to them, they are more likely to stay committed and dedicated to achieving them. This intrinsic motivation helps individuals overcome challenges and setbacks, as they are driven by a deep sense of purpose and passion for their goals. By aligning their actions and behaviors with their goals, individuals are able to cultivate a strong sense of self-discipline that enables them to overcome adversity and achieve success.

In addition, goals serve as a roadmap for personal and professional growth. By setting ambitious and challenging goals, individuals push themselves out of their comfort zones and strive for continuous improvement and development. This continuous learning and growth process helps individuals build resilience and adaptability, key traits that are essential for cultivating self-discipline. By constantly challenging themselves and pushing their limits, individuals are able to strengthen their self-discipline and develop the necessary skills and habits to overcome obstacles and achieve their goals.

Furthermore, goals can help individuals stay motivated and focused on their long-term objectives. In today's fast-paced and competitive world, it is easy to be overwhelmed by distractions and lose sight of one's goals. However, by setting clear and specific goals, individuals are able to stay motivated and

focused on their priorities. This focus enables individuals to make informed decisions and prioritize their tasks effectively, helping them stay disciplined and committed to their goals in the face of challenges and obstacles. By setting clear and meaningful goals, individuals are able to stay focused, committed, and accountable for their actions and decisions. Goals provide individuals with a sense of purpose and fulfillment, helping them cultivate a strong sense of self-discipline that enables them to overcome challenges and achieve success. Additionally, goals serve as a roadmap for personal and professional growth, helping individuals challenge themselves and strive for continuous improvement. By staying motivated and focused on their long-term objectives, individuals can develop the necessary skills and habits to cultivate self-discipline and achieve their goals.

Chapter 4: Establishing daily routines

1. THE ROLE OF CONSISTENT habits in building self-discipline

Self-discipline is a crucial element in achieving success in various aspects of life. It is the ability to control one's impulses, emotions, and behaviors in order to achieve long-term goals. Self-discipline is essential for personal growth and development, as it enables individuals to stay focused, motivated, and on track towards their objectives. One key factor that contributes to the development of self-discipline is the establishment of consistent habits.

Consistent habits play a vital role in building self-discipline because they help individuals develop a routine and structure in their lives. When individuals establish consistent habits, they are more likely to stick to a schedule and make progress towards their goals. Consistent habits create a sense of order and predictability, which can help individuals manage their time effectively and avoid distractions. By incorporating positive habits into their daily routine, individuals can develop a strong sense of self-discipline that will enable them to overcome challenges and achieve success.

Furthermore, consistent habits help individuals develop a sense of accountability and responsibility. When individuals commit to a specific habit and engage in it regularly, they are taking ownership of their actions and holding themselves accountable for their progress. This sense of responsibility can motivate individuals to stay committed to their habits and work towards their goals with perseverance and dedication. Consistent habits create a sense of structure and discipline that can help individuals navigate through obstacles and setbacks with resilience and determination.

In addition, consistent habits can help individuals build momentum and make progress towards their goals. When individuals engage in a habit consistently,

they are reinforcing positive behavior patterns and building momentum towards their objectives. Consistent habits create a sense of continuity and progress that can propel individuals towards success. By developing a routine that includes consistent habits, individuals can cultivate a strong work ethic and sense of discipline that will help them stay focused and motivated in the pursuit of their goals.

Moreover, consistent habits contribute to the development of self-control and willpower. When individuals engage in a habit consistently, they are training themselves to exercise self-control and resist temptations or distractions. Consistent habits help individuals build resilience and perseverance, enabling them to overcome challenges and obstacles with determination and strength. By establishing consistent habits and sticking to them, individuals can enhance their ability to exercise self-discipline and make positive choices that align with their long-term goals. By establishing positive habits and incorporating them into a daily routine, individuals can develop a strong sense of discipline, accountability, and responsibility. Consistent habits help individuals build momentum, make progress towards their goals, and develop self-control and willpower. By embracing consistent habits and staying committed to them, individuals can cultivate a mindset of excellence and achievement that will empower them to reach their full potential.

2. Creating a productive schedule and sticking to it

Creating a productive schedule can be a challenging but immensely rewarding task. A well-planned schedule can help you stay organized, manage your time effectively, and ultimately achieve your goals. However, the key to success lies not only in creating a schedule, but also in sticking to it consistently.

One of the first steps in creating a productive schedule is to set clear and specific goals. Before you start planning your schedule, take some time to think about what you want to achieve in the short-term and long-term. By setting clear goals, you can tailor your schedule to prioritize tasks that will help you make progress towards those goals. This will give your schedule a sense of purpose and direction, making it easier to stay motivated and focused.

Once you have defined your goals, the next step is to break them down into smaller, manageable tasks. This is where the concept of time blocking can be incredibly useful. Time blocking involves allocating specific blocks of time for different tasks or activities throughout your day. By assigning dedicated time slots for each task, you can ensure that you have a clear plan of action for how to spend your time. This can help you avoid the trap of multitasking, which can lead to decreased productivity and increased stress.

When creating your schedule, it's important to be realistic about how much time you can realistically dedicate to each task. Be sure to factor in breaks, meals, and other obligations when planning your day. Remember, it's better to underestimate how much time you need for a task and finish early, than to overestimate and feel rushed or overwhelmed.

In addition to allocating time for specific tasks, it can also be helpful to prioritize your tasks based on their urgency and importance. The Eisenhower Matrix is a useful tool for prioritizing tasks based on these two factors. Tasks that are both urgent and important should be done first, followed by tasks that are important but not urgent. Tasks that are urgent but not important can often be delegated or eliminated, while tasks that are neither urgent nor important should be put on the back burner or scheduled for a later time.

It's important to remember that creating a productive schedule is not a one-time effort, but an ongoing process. Life is unpredictable, and things don't always go according to plan. It's important to be flexible and willing to adjust your schedule as needed. If you find that certain tasks are taking longer than expected, or that unexpected priorities have come up, don't be afraid to reevaluate your schedule and make changes as necessary.

Sticking to a schedule can be challenging, especially when faced with distractions, procrastination, and unforeseen circumstances. One key to success is to develop a routine and stick to it consistently. By establishing a daily routine, you can create structure and predictability in your day, making it easier to stay on track and resist the temptation to deviate from your schedule.

Another strategy for sticking to your schedule is to eliminate distractions as much as possible. This may involve setting boundaries with friends and family, turning off notifications on your phone, or finding a quiet, designated workspace free from interruptions. By creating a conducive work environment, you can maximize your focus and productivity, making it easier to stay on task and accomplish your goals.

Procrastination is another common obstacle to sticking to a schedule. One way to combat procrastination is to break tasks down into smaller, more manageable steps. By setting achievable milestones and rewarding yourself for completing them, you can build momentum and create a sense of accomplishment that can help you stay motivated and on track.

All in all, it's important to remember that self-care is an essential component of productivity. It's easy to fall into the trap of overworking and neglecting your physical and mental well-being. However, taking care of yourself is crucial for maintaining a productive schedule in the long run. Be sure to prioritize rest, exercise, healthy eating, and relaxation to ensure that you have the energy and focus necessary to stick to your schedule and achieve your goals. By setting clear goals, prioritizing tasks, establishing a routine, eliminating distractions, combating procrastination, and practicing self-care, you can create a schedule that works for you and help you achieve success in your personal and professional endeavors. Remember, consistency is key, so stay committed to your schedule and be willing to adapt and make adjustments as needed. With dedication and perseverance, you can maximize your productivity and reach your full potential.

3. Tips for overcoming procrastination and distractions

Overcoming procrastination and distractions can be a challenging feat for many individuals, as it requires discipline, self-awareness, and a willingness to change unproductive habits. Procrastination is defined as the act of delaying or postponing tasks that need to be accomplished, while distractions are external stimuli that divert one's attention away from their intended focus. Both procrastination and distractions can hinder productivity, decrease motivation, and contribute to feelings of stress and overwhelm. However, by implementing

effective strategies and techniques, individuals can learn to overcome these obstacles and improve their ability to stay focused, set goals, and manage their time efficiently.

One key tip for overcoming procrastination is to break tasks down into smaller, more manageable steps. Oftentimes, procrastination occurs when a task feels overwhelming or daunting. By breaking tasks down into smaller, more achievable steps, individuals can reduce feelings of overwhelm and increase their motivation to get started. For example, if a student has a research paper due in two weeks, they can break the task down into smaller steps such as conducting research, creating an outline, writing a rough draft, and revising and editing the final paper. This approach helps to create a clear roadmap for completing the task and makes it easier to get started.

Another helpful tip for overcoming procrastination is to create a structured schedule or routine. Having a set schedule for when tasks will be completed can help individuals stay on track and avoid the temptation to procrastinate. This can be achieved by using tools such as calendars, planners, or to-do lists to plan out daily or weekly tasks and deadlines. By allocating specific blocks of time for each task, individuals can create a sense of urgency and accountability that can help them stay focused and motivated to complete their work in a timely manner. Additionally, incorporating regular breaks and rewards into the schedule can help prevent burnout and maintain motivation throughout the day.

In addition to breaking tasks down and creating a structured schedule, another valuable tip for overcoming procrastination is to eliminate distractions. Distractions can come in many forms, such as social media, emails, notifications, or noise. By identifying common distractions and taking steps to minimize or eliminate them, individuals can create a more conducive environment for focus and concentration. This can involve turning off notifications, setting boundaries with others, working in a quiet or secluded space, or using productivity tools such as website blockers or time management apps to limit distractions. By creating a distraction-free work environment, individuals can improve their ability to stay on task and complete their work efficiently.

Furthermore, setting specific goals and deadlines can be an effective strategy for overcoming procrastination and increasing motivation. By setting clear, measurable goals and deadlines, individuals can create a sense of purpose and direction that can help them stay motivated and on track. This can involve setting both short-term and long-term goals, breaking larger goals into smaller milestones, and tracking progress regularly to stay accountable. By setting deadlines for each task or milestone, individuals can create a sense of urgency that can help them stay focused and prioritize their work effectively. Additionally, sharing goals with others or seeking accountability can provide external motivation and support to help individuals stay on track and overcome procrastination.

Lastly, practicing self-care and maintaining a healthy work-life balance is essential for overcoming procrastination and distractions. Taking care of one's physical and mental well-being can improve focus, energy levels, and overall productivity. This can involve getting an adequate amount of sleep, eating nutritious foods, staying active, and practicing stress-reducing activities such as mindfulness, meditation, or exercise. Additionally, taking regular breaks, setting aside time for relaxation and leisure activities, and maintaining social connections can help individuals recharge and prevent burnout. By prioritizing self-care and finding a balance between work and personal life, individuals can improve their ability to stay focused, motivated, and productive in the face of procrastination and distractions. However, by implementing effective strategies such as breaking tasks down, creating a structured schedule, eliminating distractions, setting goals and deadlines, and practicing self-care, individuals can improve their ability to stay focused, motivated, and productive. By making small changes to their habits and routines, individuals can overcome procrastination, increase their productivity, and achieve their goals with greater ease and success.

Chapter 5: Managing time effectively

1. PRIORITIZING TASKS and activities to optimize time management

Time management is a crucial skill that can have a significant impact on one's productivity and overall success. In today's fast-paced world, it is more important than ever to prioritize tasks and activities in order to make the most efficient use of our time. By effectively managing our time, we can reduce stress, increase productivity, and achieve our goals more quickly and effectively.

The first step in prioritizing tasks and activities is to assess the importance and urgency of each task. This can be done by creating a prioritization matrix, in which tasks are divided into four categories: urgent and important, important but not urgent, urgent but not important, and neither urgent nor important. By categorizing tasks in this way, we can more easily determine which tasks require immediate attention and which can be postponed or delegated.

Once tasks have been categorized, it is important to create a to-do list or schedule that clearly outlines the order in which tasks should be completed. This can help to ensure that the most important tasks are completed first, while also allowing for flexibility in case unexpected tasks or emergencies arise. By breaking tasks down into smaller, manageable steps, we can also avoid feeling overwhelmed and make progress more quickly.

Another key aspect of optimizing time management is setting realistic goals and deadlines for tasks. By establishing clear objectives and timelines, we can create a sense of accountability and motivation to complete tasks in a timely manner. It is important to be realistic about the time and resources required to complete each task, and to adjust our goals as needed based on our progress and changing priorities.

In addition to setting goals and deadlines, it is also important to eliminate distractions and time-wasting activities that can detract from our productivity. This can involve setting boundaries with colleagues or family members, turning off notifications on our devices, or finding a quiet and organized workspace where we can focus on our tasks without interruptions. By minimizing distractions, we can increase our efficiency and concentration, allowing us to complete tasks more quickly and effectively.

To recapitulate, it is important to regularly review and reassess our priorities in order to ensure that we are making the most efficient use of our time. This can involve reflecting on our goals, identifying any tasks that are no longer relevant or necessary, and adjusting our priorities as needed. By regularly reviewing and updating our to-do lists and schedules, we can stay on track and make progress towards our goals in a more organized and efficient manner. By categorizing tasks, creating to-do lists, setting goals and deadlines, eliminating distractions, and regularly reviewing our priorities, we can make the most efficient use of our time and achieve our goals more effectively. By taking a proactive and strategic approach to time management, we can reduce stress, increase productivity, and ultimately achieve greater success in both our personal and professional lives.

2. Techniques for improving focus and concentration

In today's fast-paced world, the ability to focus and concentrate is more important than ever. Whether you are a student trying to study for an exam, a professional working on a project, or simply trying to stay on task in your daily life, having a strong ability to focus can make a significant difference in your success. Fortunately, there are several techniques that can help improve your focus and concentration, allowing you to work more efficiently and effectively.

One of the most effective techniques for improving focus and concentration is mindfulness meditation. Mindfulness meditation involves focusing your attention on the present moment, without judgment or distraction. By practicing mindfulness meditation regularly, you can train your brain to stay focused on the task at hand, rather than getting sidetracked by thoughts or distractions. Research has shown that mindfulness meditation can improve

attention and focus, as well as reduce stress and anxiety, making it a valuable tool for improving concentration.

Another technique for improving focus and concentration is to break tasks down into smaller, more manageable pieces. When faced with a large or complex task, it can be easy to feel overwhelmed and lose focus. By breaking the task down into smaller steps, you can make it more manageable and easier to stay focused. This technique, known as chunking, can help improve your ability to concentrate on each individual step, rather than getting overwhelmed by the overall task. By focusing on one step at a time, you can stay on track and make progress towards completing the task.

Exercise is another important technique for improving focus and concentration. Regular physical activity has been shown to boost cognitive function, including attention and focus. Exercise increases blood flow to the brain, which can help improve concentration and mental clarity. In addition, exercise releases endorphins, which can reduce stress and improve mood, making it easier to stay focused and on task. Whether you prefer running, yoga, or weightlifting, incorporating regular exercise into your routine can help improve your ability to concentrate and stay focused throughout the day.

Keeping a tidy and organized workspace can also help improve focus and concentration. A cluttered or disorganized environment can be distracting and make it difficult to focus on the task at hand. By keeping your workspace clean and organized, you can create a more conducive environment for concentration. This can include decluttering your desk, organizing your files and supplies, and minimizing distractions such as noise or visual clutter. By creating a space that is conducive to focus, you can improve your ability to concentrate on your work and stay on task.

Ultimately, practicing good time management skills can help improve focus and concentration. By setting clear goals and deadlines, prioritizing tasks, and breaking larger tasks into smaller steps, you can create a more structured and organized approach to your work. This can help you stay focused and on track, rather than feeling overwhelmed or distracted by competing priorities. By planning your day and allocating time for specific tasks, you can reduce

procrastination and improve your ability to concentrate on the task at hand. Additionally, taking regular breaks and scheduling time for rest and relaxation can help prevent burnout and maintain focus throughout the day. By incorporating mindfulness meditation, breaking tasks into smaller steps, exercising regularly, keeping a tidy workspace, and practicing good time management skills, you can enhance your ability to stay focused and on task. These techniques can help improve cognitive function, reduce stress, and increase productivity, ultimately leading to greater success in your endeavors. By making a conscious effort to prioritize focus and concentration, you can enhance your performance and achieve your goals more effectively.

3. The link between time management and self-discipline

Time management and self-discipline are two interconnected concepts that play a crucial role in our daily lives. Time management refers to the process of planning and organizing how to divide your time between specific activities. On the other hand, self-discipline is the ability to control your impulses, emotions, and actions to achieve a desired goal. These two concepts go hand in hand, as effective time management requires a high level of self-discipline to stick to your schedule and prioritize tasks. In this paragraph, we will explore the link between time management and self-discipline, and how they can impact your overall productivity and success.

One of the key reasons why time management and self-discipline are closely linked is that they both require self-awareness and introspection. To effectively manage your time, you need to have a clear understanding of your goals, priorities, and daily activities. This requires self-discipline to set aside time for important tasks and avoid distractions. Self-discipline also plays a crucial role in sticking to your schedule and resisting the temptation to procrastinate. Without self-discipline, it can be challenging to prioritize tasks and make the most of your time.

Furthermore, time management and self-discipline are essential skills for achieving long-term goals and success. By effectively managing your time and practicing self-discipline, you can improve your productivity, create a sense of accomplishment, and reach your full potential. When you have the discipline

to stay focused and prioritize tasks, you can make progress towards your goals and achieve success in your personal and professional life. Time management helps you allocate your time wisely, while self-discipline helps you stay committed to your goals and overcome obstacles that may come your way.

In addition, time management and self-discipline can also contribute to a better work-life balance. By effectively managing your time and practicing self-discipline, you can create more time for yourself, your family, and your hobbies. This can reduce stress, improve your overall well-being, and help you maintain a healthy balance between your personal and professional life. When you have a clear understanding of your priorities and effectively manage your time, you can create more opportunities to enjoy the things that matter most to you, leading to a happier and more fulfilling life.

Moreover, time management and self-discipline are essential skills for achieving success in the workplace. Employers value employees who can manage their time effectively, prioritize tasks, and stay focused on their goals. By practicing self-discipline and sticking to your schedule, you can demonstrate your reliability, commitment, and ability to meet deadlines. This can lead to greater opportunities for career advancement, increased job satisfaction, and higher levels of productivity and efficiency. Time management and self-discipline are key components of professional success and can help you stand out in a competitive job market. By effectively managing your time and practicing self-discipline, you can achieve your goals, maintain a healthy work-life balance, and succeed in your personal and professional life. It is important to develop these skills through practice, self-awareness, and commitment. With dedication and effort, you can improve your time management and self-discipline skills, and unlock your full potential for success.

Chapter 6: Developing self-control

1. UNDERSTANDING IMPULSES and learning to control them

Impulses are innate reactions that drive us to act without much consideration for the consequences. These impulses can manifest in various forms, such as sudden urges to eat a slice of cake or buy a new gadget. While impulses are a normal part of human behavior, learning to control them is crucial for maintaining self-control and making rational decisions.

One of the first steps in understanding impulses is to recognize their triggers. Impulses are often triggered by external stimuli, such as advertisements, social media, or peer pressure. By becoming aware of these triggers, we can begin to identify patterns in our impulses and gain insight into their underlying causes. For example, someone who consistently feels the urge to shop online may realize that their impulses are triggered by feelings of boredom or stress.

Once we have identified the triggers of our impulses, we can begin to implement strategies to control them. One effective strategy is to pause and reflect before acting on an impulse. Taking a moment to consider the potential consequences of our actions can help us make more rational decisions and avoid acting impulsively. Another strategy is to distract ourselves from the impulse by engaging in a different activity or focusing on a different task. For example, someone who is tempted to indulge in unhealthy snacks may choose to go for a walk or read a book instead.

In addition to external triggers, impulses can also be influenced by internal factors such as emotions and habits. Emotions such as anxiety, frustration, or excitement can amplify impulses and make them harder to resist. By learning to regulate our emotions and practicing mindfulness, we can reduce the intensity of our impulses and make it easier to control them. Furthermore, breaking

harmful habits that reinforce our impulses, such as overeating or overspending, can help us gain control over our actions.

It is important to note that learning to control impulses is a gradual process that requires patience and practice. It is normal to experience setbacks along the way, but it is important to learn from these setbacks and continue working towards self-control. Developing a support system of friends, family, or a therapist can also be beneficial in helping us navigate the challenges of impulse control. By recognizing the triggers of our impulses, implementing strategies to control them, regulating our emotions, and breaking harmful habits, we can empower ourselves to make conscious choices and resist the urge to act impulsively. While the process of controlling impulses may be challenging, it is ultimately rewarding and can lead to greater self-awareness and personal growth.

2. Strategies for managing emotions and impulses

Managing emotions and impulses is a critical aspect of emotional intelligence that can greatly impact our personal and professional lives. Emotions play a significant role in decision-making, communication, and relationships, and being able to effectively manage them can lead to better outcomes and more positive interactions. In this article, we will explore some strategies for managing emotions and impulses that can help individuals navigate challenging situations and enhance their overall well-being.

One of the key strategies for managing emotions and impulses is self-awareness. Understanding your own emotions and recognizing how they influence your thoughts and behaviors is essential for effective emotional regulation. By increasing your awareness of your emotional triggers and patterns, you can begin to develop strategies for managing them more effectively. This might involve taking time to reflect on your feelings, journaling about your emotions, or seeking feedback from trusted individuals to gain insight into how you are perceived by others.

Another important strategy for managing emotions and impulses is practicing emotional regulation skills. This involves learning how to control your

emotional responses in different situations and not letting your feelings dictate your actions. Techniques such as deep breathing, mindfulness, and cognitive reframing can help you stay calm and rational in the face of strong emotions. By practicing these skills regularly, you can improve your ability to manage your impulses and make more thoughtful decisions.

It is also helpful to build strong social connections and support systems to help you manage your emotions effectively. Having a network of friends, family, or colleagues who can provide emotional support and perspective can be invaluable in times of stress or uncertainty. Being able to talk openly about your feelings and receive validation and encouragement from others can help you process your emotions and gain a more balanced perspective on challenging situations.

In addition to self-awareness and emotional regulation, setting boundaries and practicing self-care are essential strategies for managing emotions and impulses. Setting healthy boundaries in your relationships and work environment can help you protect your emotional well-being and prevent others from triggering negative emotions or impulsive reactions. Taking care of yourself through activities such as exercise, meditation, hobbies, and relaxation can also help you manage stress and maintain a positive outlook, reducing the likelihood of emotional outbursts or impulsive behavior.

To summarize, seeking professional help or counseling can be beneficial for individuals who are struggling to manage their emotions and impulses effectively. A trained therapist or counselor can provide guidance, support, and skills training to help you understand and regulate your emotions more effectively. Therapy can also help you explore underlying issues or trauma that may be contributing to your struggles with emotional regulation, helping you to address and overcome these challenges in a healthy and sustainable way. By practicing self-awareness, emotional regulation, building social support, setting boundaries, practicing self-care, and seeking professional help when needed, individuals can enhance their emotional intelligence and develop strategies for managing their emotions effectively. By implementing these strategies in our daily lives, we can improve our relationships, decision-making, and overall quality of life.

3. Practicing mindfulness and self-awareness techniques

Practicing mindfulness and self-awareness techniques is an essential aspect of personal development and mental well-being. These practices involve being fully present in the moment, paying attention to our thoughts, emotions, and bodily sensations without judgment. Through mindfulness, individuals can cultivate a deeper awareness of their thoughts and feelings, allowing them to respond to situations in a more thoughtful and deliberate manner.

One of the key benefits of practicing mindfulness is the ability to reduce stress and anxiety. By focusing on the present moment and letting go of worries about the past or future, individuals can experience a sense of calm and tranquility. This can help to alleviate feelings of overwhelm and promote a greater sense of mental clarity.

Self-awareness is closely linked to mindfulness, as it involves recognizing and understanding our own thoughts, emotions, and behaviors. By developing self-awareness, individuals can gain insight into their motivations and values, allowing them to make more informed decisions and navigate challenging situations more effectively. Self-awareness can also help individuals identify patterns of behavior that may be holding them back or causing difficulties in their lives, allowing them to make positive changes and grow as individuals.

There are many techniques that can be used to cultivate mindfulness and self-awareness. One common practice is meditation, which involves focusing on the breath or a specific object to quiet the mind and increase awareness of the present moment. Mindful breathing exercises can also help individuals to center themselves and bring their attention back to the present when they are feeling stressed or overwhelmed.

Another effective technique for developing mindfulness and self-awareness is journaling. By regularly writing down our thoughts and feelings, we can gain insight into our emotional patterns and triggers, as well as identify areas of our lives that may need attention or improvement. Journaling can also be a therapeutic way to process difficult emotions and experiences, allowing us to

release negative energy and move forward with greater clarity and self-understanding.

In addition to meditation and journaling, mindfulness can also be practiced through daily activities such as eating, walking, or even washing dishes. By bringing our full attention to these simple tasks, we can cultivate a greater sense of presence and awareness in our daily lives. This can help us to appreciate the beauty and richness of each moment, as well as stay grounded and focused in the face of life's challenges. By cultivating these skills, we can learn to respond to difficult situations with grace and equanimity, as well as develop a deeper understanding of ourselves and our relationships with others. Through regular practice and dedication, we can cultivate a greater sense of inner peace and fulfillment, allowing us to live more authentically and joyfully in the present moment.

Chapter 7: Cultivating self-motivation

1. FINDING INTRINSIC sources of motivation

Finding intrinsic sources of motivation is a key component of achieving success in any endeavor. Intrinsic motivation refers to the internal drive that fuels our actions and behaviors, as opposed to extrinsic motivation which comes from external rewards or punishments. While extrinsic motivation can be effective in the short term, it is often not sustainable in the long run. Intrinsic motivation, on the other hand, is more powerful and enduring because it comes from within ourselves.

One of the ways to cultivate intrinsic motivation is by setting meaningful goals that align with our values and interests. When we have a clear sense of purpose and direction, we are more likely to stay motivated and focused on our objectives. It is important to take the time to reflect on what truly matters to us and to identify our core values. By aligning our goals with these values, we can tap into a deep well of intrinsic motivation that will sustain us through challenges and setbacks.

Another important factor in finding intrinsic sources of motivation is to cultivate a growth mindset. A growth mindset is the belief that our abilities and intelligence can be developed through effort and practice. When we approach challenges with a growth mindset, we are more likely to stay motivated and resilient in the face of obstacles. By viewing failure as an opportunity to learn and grow, we can maintain a positive attitude and a sense of optimism that will fuel our motivation.

Self-awareness is also crucial in finding intrinsic sources of motivation. By understanding our strengths and weaknesses, as well as our likes and dislikes, we can tailor our goals and activities to suit our individual preferences and abilities. When we engage in activities that resonate with our interests and passions, we

are more likely to experience a sense of flow, or deep absorption in our tasks, which can be highly motivating.

Building a supportive environment is another key factor in cultivating intrinsic motivation. Surrounding ourselves with positive and encouraging people who share our values and aspirations can provide us with the support and motivation we need to stay focused on our goals. By seeking out mentors and role models who inspire us, we can learn from their experiences and insights, and draw strength from their encouragement and guidance.

Lastly, it is important to celebrate our successes along the way. By recognizing and acknowledging our progress and achievements, we can boost our confidence and motivation to keep moving forward. Taking the time to reflect on how far we have come and to appreciate our accomplishments can fuel our desire to continue pursuing our goals with passion and determination. By tapping into our internal drive and staying true to our values and passions, we can sustain our motivation and energy over the long term, and achieve the success and fulfillment we desire.

2. Setting rewards and incentives to stay motivated

As human beings, we are naturally inclined to seek out rewards and incentives in order to stay motivated and engaged in our activities. Whether it is in the workplace, at school, or in our personal lives, having a system in place that acknowledges and rewards our efforts can significantly impact our performance and overall satisfaction. In this discussion, we will explore the importance of setting rewards and incentives to stay motivated, as well as examine some effective strategies for implementing them in various settings.

One of the key reasons why setting rewards and incentives is essential for motivation is that it provides us with a clear sense of purpose and direction. When we know that there is something to be gained from our hard work and dedication, we are more likely to put in the effort required to achieve our goals. This can be particularly important in the workplace, where employees may need an extra push to go above and beyond in their duties. By offering rewards such as bonuses, promotions, or even simple recognition for a job well

done, organizations can create a sense of motivation and drive among their employees.

Furthermore, rewards and incentives can help to reinforce positive behaviors and habits. When we are rewarded for demonstrating certain qualities or skills, we are more likely to continue exhibiting those behaviors in the future. This can be particularly useful in educational settings, where students can be motivated to work harder and achieve better results when they are offered incentives such as prizes or praise for their efforts. By acknowledging and rewarding desired behaviors, teachers can create a positive learning environment that encourages students to excel and reach their full potential.

In addition to providing motivation and reinforcing positive behaviors, setting rewards and incentives can also help to boost morale and enhance overall satisfaction. When we feel appreciated and recognized for our contributions, we are more likely to feel valued and engaged in our work or activities. This can lead to higher levels of job satisfaction, increased productivity, and a greater sense of fulfillment in what we do. In a world where burnout and disengagement are becoming increasingly common, it is crucial for organizations to create a culture that values and rewards its employees for their hard work and dedication.

When it comes to setting rewards and incentives, there are a variety of strategies that can be effective in different situations. In the workplace, for example, organizations can offer financial rewards such as bonuses, raises, or profit-sharing programs to motivate employees to perform at their best. Additionally, non-monetary incentives such as extra vacation days, flexible work hours, or opportunities for career advancement can also be highly motivating for employees. By offering a combination of both financial and non-financial rewards, organizations can cater to the diverse needs and motivations of their workforce.

In educational settings, teachers can implement a variety of rewards and incentives to motivate students and encourage their success. These can include tangible rewards such as prizes, certificates, or special privileges for achieving certain goals or milestones. Additionally, teachers can also provide intangible

rewards such as praise, encouragement, or positive feedback to reinforce desired behaviors and attitudes. By creating a reward system that is tailored to the needs and preferences of their students, teachers can help to create a positive learning environment that fosters motivation and engagement. Whether in the workplace, at school, or in our personal lives, having a system in place that acknowledges and rewards our efforts can have a significant impact on our performance and overall satisfaction. By providing clear goals, reinforcing positive behaviors, and boosting morale, rewards and incentives can help us to achieve our full potential and reach our goals. By implementing effective strategies for setting rewards and incentives, we can create a culture of motivation and excellence that fosters success and fulfillment in all aspects of our lives.

3. Overcoming demotivation and staying on track

Demotivation is a common struggle that many individuals face in their personal and professional lives. It can manifest in various forms, such as feeling overwhelmed, lacking enthusiasm, or experiencing a lack of purpose or direction. However, it is essential to recognize that demotivation is a natural and temporary part of the human experience. It is not a sign of failure or weakness, but rather a signal that something is amiss and needs to be addressed.

One of the first steps in overcoming demotivation is to identify the root cause of your feelings. This may involve reflecting on your current circumstances, goals, and priorities, as well as exploring any underlying fears, insecurities, or uncertainties that may be contributing to your lack of motivation. By gaining a deeper understanding of what is holding you back, you can begin to develop strategies for moving forward and regaining your sense of purpose and drive.

Another key factor in overcoming demotivation is setting realistic and achievable goals for yourself. This may involve breaking down larger objectives into smaller, manageable tasks, creating a timeline for completion, and establishing a system for tracking your progress. By setting clear and specific goals, you can create a sense of direction and momentum that can help you stay on track and motivated in the long term.

It is also important to surround yourself with a supportive network of friends, family, mentors, and colleagues who can provide encouragement, advice, and accountability. Building relationships with like-minded individuals who share your values and goals can help you stay motivated and focused, as well as provide you with a sense of belonging and connection. By seeking out support from others, you can create a sense of community and collaboration that can help you overcome challenges and obstacles.

In addition to seeking support from others, it is crucial to prioritize self-care and well-being in your journey to overcome demotivation. This may involve incorporating regular exercise, healthy eating, and relaxation techniques into your daily routine, as well as engaging in activities that bring you joy and fulfillment. By taking care of your physical, mental, and emotional health, you can build resilience and strength that can help you navigate the ups and downs of life with greater ease and confidence.

It is also important to cultivate a growth mindset and embrace failure as a learning opportunity. Instead of viewing setbacks and obstacles as insurmountable barriers, try to reframe them as valuable lessons that can help you grow, develop, and improve. By adopting a positive and resilient attitude towards challenges, you can build the resilience and determination needed to stay motivated and on track in the face of adversity.

All in all, it is essential to celebrate your accomplishments and milestones along the way. By acknowledging and rewarding your progress, no matter how small, you can boost your confidence and motivation, as well as remind yourself of your capabilities and potential. Whether it's treating yourself to a small indulgence, sharing your achievements with others, or simply taking a moment to reflect on your growth and progress, celebrating your successes can help you stay on track and motivated in the long term. By taking proactive steps to address the root causes of your demotivation, set realistic goals, seek support from others, prioritize self-care, embrace failure as a learning opportunity, and celebrate your achievements, you can build the resilience and determination needed to overcome challenges and obstacles and stay motivated and focused on your path to success. Remember, demotivation is a natural and temporary

part of the human experience, and with the right tools and strategies, you can navigate through it with grace, confidence, and determination.

Chapter 8: Building resilience

1. UNDERSTANDING THE value of resilience in facing setbacks and challenges

Resilience is a crucial trait that plays a significant role in helping individuals navigate through setbacks and challenges that they may face in their lives. It is the ability to bounce back from difficult experiences and adapt in the face of adversity. Resilience is not only important in overcoming obstacles, but it also helps individuals grow stronger and more capable of handling future difficulties. In today's fast-paced and unpredictable world, being resilient can make a real difference in how we handle setbacks and move forward in a positive direction.

When we face setbacks and challenges, it is natural to feel overwhelmed, stressed, and discouraged. However, resilience allows us to acknowledge our feelings and emotions, but also to look for ways to overcome the obstacles in our path. Resilient individuals are able to find solutions to problems, learn from their experiences, and make the necessary changes to improve their situations. They have a growth mindset that allows them to see setbacks as opportunities for growth and development, rather than insurmountable barriers.

One of the key components of resilience is the ability to adapt to change. Life is full of unexpected twists and turns, and being able to adjust to new circumstances is essential for overcoming challenges. Resilient individuals are flexible and open-minded, willing to try new strategies and approaches in order to succeed. They are not afraid to seek help from others or learn from their mistakes, recognizing that failure is a natural part of the learning process. By staying open to new possibilities and remaining adaptable, resilient individuals are better equipped to face setbacks and emerge stronger on the other side.

Another important aspect of resilience is having a strong support system in place. When we face challenges, having friends, family, or mentors to lean on can make a big difference in how we cope and overcome adversity. Supportive relationships provide us with encouragement, guidance, and a sense of belonging that can boost our resilience and help us stay strong in difficult times. By surrounding ourselves with people who care about our well-being and believe in our ability to overcome obstacles, we can fuel our resilience and face challenges with confidence and determination.

Furthermore, resilience is also closely tied to self-care and well-being. Taking care of ourselves physically, emotionally, and mentally is essential for building resilience and developing the strength to face setbacks. Eating well, exercising regularly, getting enough sleep, and practicing mindfulness are all ways to nourish our bodies and minds, making us better equipped to handle stress and adversity. Additionally, engaging in activities that bring joy and fulfillment, such as hobbies, creative pursuits, or spending time in nature, can help boost our resilience and restore our energy when facing challenges. By developing resilience, we can learn to bounce back from difficult experiences, adapt to change, seek support from others, and practice self-care to build our inner strength and fortitude. In today's uncertain and complex world, resilience is more important than ever in helping us overcome obstacles and thrive in the face of adversity. So let us embrace resilience as a key tool in facing challenges and setbacks, and strive to cultivate this important trait in our lives for a brighter, more resilient future.

2. Strategies for bouncing back from failures and disappointments

In our professional and personal lives, we encounter setbacks, failures, and disappointments on a regular basis. These experiences can be difficult to navigate, but they also provide valuable opportunities for growth and resilience. Developing effective strategies for bouncing back from failures and disappointments is essential for achieving success and maintaining a positive outlook in the face of adversity.

One key strategy for bouncing back from failures and disappointments is to reframe setbacks as learning opportunities. Rather than viewing failure as a reflection of one's abilities or worth, it can be helpful to see it as a chance to learn, grow, and improve. By reframing failure in this way, individuals can shift their perspective and focus on the lessons that can be gleaned from the experience. This can help to foster a growth mindset, where obstacles are seen as opportunities for development rather than impediments to success.

Another important strategy for bouncing back from failures and disappointments is to practice self-compassion. It is easy to be hard on ourselves when we experience setbacks, but self-compassion involves treating ourselves with kindness and understanding, especially in times of difficulty. By practicing self-compassion, individuals can cultivate a sense of resilience and emotional strength that allows them to bounce back from failures and disappointments more effectively. This involves acknowledging and validating one's feelings of disappointment or frustration, while also offering oneself support and encouragement.

Additionally, setting realistic goals and expectations can help individuals bounce back from failures and disappointments. By setting achievable goals and avoiding perfectionism, individuals can better manage their expectations and reduce the likelihood of experiencing setbacks. When goals are realistic, individuals are more likely to feel a sense of accomplishment and progress, even in the face of challenges. This can help to build resilience and foster a positive attitude, which can be instrumental in bouncing back from failures and disappointments.

Moreover, seeking support from friends, family, or colleagues can be a valuable strategy for bouncing back from failures and disappointments. In times of difficulty, having a strong support network can provide emotional and practical support, as well as a sense of belonging and connection. Talking about one's experiences with others can help to gain new perspectives, advice, and encouragement, which can be instrumental in overcoming setbacks. It is important to remember that seeking support is not a sign of weakness, but rather a sign of strength and resilience.

Furthermore, practicing mindfulness and self-care can also be helpful in bouncing back from failures and disappointments. Mindfulness involves being present in the moment and paying attention to one's thoughts and feelings without judgment. By practicing mindfulness, individuals can cultivate a sense of calm, clarity, and perspective that can help them navigate challenges more effectively. Engaging in self-care activities, such as exercise, meditation, or hobbies, can also help individuals recharge and refocus, allowing them to bounce back from failures and disappointments with renewed energy and resilience. By reframing setbacks as learning opportunities, practicing self-compassion, setting realistic goals and expectations, seeking support, and practicing mindfulness and self-care, individuals can cultivate resilience and emotional strength that allows them to bounce back from failures and disappointments more effectively. These strategies can help individuals navigate challenges, setbacks, and disappointments with grace and resilience, ultimately leading to personal and professional growth and success.

3. Cultivating a growth mindset to enhance resilience

Developing a growth mindset is essential for enhancing resilience in individuals. A growth mindset is the belief that abilities and intelligence can be developed through dedication and hard work. This mindset contrasts with a fixed mindset, where individuals believe that their abilities are fixed and cannot be changed. By cultivating a growth mindset, individuals are more likely to persevere through challenges and setbacks, as they see them as opportunities for growth and learning rather than limitations. This mindset encourages individuals to embrace challenges, learn from criticism, and persist in the face of obstacles.

One way to cultivate a growth mindset is to embrace challenges. Challenges are an inevitable part of life, and individuals with a growth mindset see them as opportunities for growth and learning. Instead of avoiding challenges out of fear of failure, individuals with a growth mindset are willing to take on new challenges and learn from their experiences. By embracing challenges, individuals can develop resilience and a greater sense of self-efficacy, which can help them overcome obstacles in the future.

Another way to develop a growth mindset is to learn from criticism. Instead of taking criticism personally and viewing it as a reflection of their abilities, individuals with a growth mindset see it as an opportunity for improvement. By viewing criticism as constructive feedback, individuals can learn from their mistakes and make changes to improve their performance. This willingness to learn and grow from feedback is essential for developing resilience and overcoming challenges.

Persistence is another key component of developing a growth mindset. Individuals with a growth mindset understand that success is not always immediate and that progress takes time and effort. Instead of giving up in the face of failure, individuals with a growth mindset persist in their efforts and continue to work towards their goals. This persistence can help individuals develop resilience and the ability to overcome obstacles.

In addition to embracing challenges, learning from criticism, and persisting in their efforts, individuals can also develop a growth mindset by seeking out opportunities for growth and learning. This can involve taking on new challenges, seeking feedback from others, and engaging in lifelong learning. By actively seeking out opportunities for growth, individuals can develop the skills and abilities needed to overcome challenges and build resilience. By embracing challenges, learning from criticism, persisting in their efforts, and seeking out opportunities for growth and learning, individuals can develop the mindset needed to overcome obstacles and thrive in the face of adversity. With a growth mindset, individuals can develop the resilience and determination needed to succeed in both their personal and professional lives.

Chapter 9: Practicing self-care

1. THE ROLE OF SELF-care in maintaining mental and physical well-being

Self-care is a term that is often thrown around in discussions about health and wellness, but what exactly does it mean and why is it important. Self-care refers to the practice of taking care of oneself in order to maintain physical, mental, and emotional well-being. It encompasses a wide range of activities, from getting enough sleep and exercise to practicing mindfulness and setting boundaries with others. The importance of self-care cannot be overstated, as it plays a crucial role in maintaining mental and physical health.

In today's fast-paced and demanding world, many people neglect their own well-being in favor of meeting the needs of others or achieving their goals. This can lead to burnout, stress, and even physical illness. By taking the time to prioritize self-care, individuals can prevent these negative consequences and improve their overall quality of life. Self-care is not a selfish act, but rather a necessary one in order to be able to show up fully for oneself and others.

One of the key ways in which self-care contributes to mental well-being is through stress management. Stress is a normal part of life, but when it becomes chronic or overwhelming, it can have serious consequences for both mental and physical health. By engaging in self-care activities such as exercise, meditation, or spending time in nature, individuals can reduce their stress levels and improve their mental resilience. This in turn can lead to better mood regulation, increased focus and concentration, and a greater sense of overall well-being.

Physical well-being is also closely linked to self-care practices. Taking care of one's body through regular exercise, nutritious diet, and sufficient sleep is essential for maintaining physical health. These basic self-care practices can

help prevent chronic illnesses such as heart disease, diabetes, and obesity, as well as improving overall energy levels and longevity. In addition to these fundamental practices, self-care can also include activities such as getting regular check-ups with healthcare providers, taking time off when needed, and seeking support when facing health challenges.

In addition to the physical and mental benefits of self-care, it also plays a key role in fostering emotional well-being. Emotions are an important part of the human experience, and taking care of one's emotional health is just as important as taking care of one's physical and mental health. Self-care practices can help individuals cultivate self-awareness, emotional regulation, and resilience in the face of life's challenges. By engaging in activities that bring joy, fulfillment, and connection, individuals can nurture their emotional well-being and enhance their overall quality of life.

It's important to note that self-care is not a one-size-fits-all approach. What works for one person may not work for another, and individuals may need to experiment with different self-care practices to find what truly resonates with them. It's also important to prioritize self-care on a regular basis, rather than waiting until burnout or illness force us to take action. By making self-care a part of our daily routine, we can proactively support our mental and physical well-being and lead healthier, happier lives. By prioritizing activities that support our physical, mental, and emotional health, we can prevent burnout, reduce stress, and improve overall quality of life. Self-care is not a luxury, but a necessity for leading a healthy and fulfilling life. By taking the time to care for ourselves, we can show up fully for ourselves and others, and thrive in all areas of our lives.

2. Strategies for managing stress and avoiding burnout

Stress is a common experience for many individuals, especially those in high-pressure situations or demanding professions. While some level of stress can be motivating and help individuals perform at their best, chronic stress can lead to burnout, which can have serious consequences on one's physical and mental health. Burnout is characterized by exhaustion, cynicism, and reduced

professional efficacy. It can lead to decreased productivity, dissatisfaction with work, and even long-term health problems.

In order to avoid burnout and manage stress effectively, it is important for individuals to develop strategies that help them cope with the demands of their daily lives. One key strategy is to prioritize self-care and make time for activities that promote relaxation and rejuvenation. This can include activities such as exercise, meditation, mindfulness, and spending time in nature. Engaging in these activities can help individuals recharge and reduce the negative effects of stress on their bodies and minds.

Another important strategy for managing stress is to set boundaries and learn to say no when necessary. It can be tempting to take on too much and try to please everyone, but this can lead to overwhelming levels of stress and burnout. By setting boundaries and prioritizing tasks, individuals can better manage their time and focus on activities that are most important to them. Learning to say no when necessary can also help individuals avoid overextending themselves and maintain a healthy work-life balance.

In addition to setting boundaries, it is important for individuals to practice self-awareness and recognize the early signs of stress and burnout. By being attuned to their own emotions and physical sensations, individuals can take proactive steps to address stress before it escalates into burnout. This can involve taking breaks when needed, seeking social support, and engaging in stress-reducing activities. By recognizing and responding to early signs of stress, individuals can prevent burnout and maintain their well-being.

It is also helpful for individuals to cultivate a support network of friends, family members, and colleagues who can provide emotional support and encouragement during times of stress. Having a strong support system can help individuals feel less isolated and overwhelmed, and can provide a sounding board for discussing stressors and finding solutions. Building strong relationships with others can also help individuals feel more connected and supported, which can buffer against the negative effects of stress.

In short, it is important for individuals to practice good self-care habits, such as getting enough sleep, eating a balanced diet, and staying physically active. Sleep deprivation, poor nutrition, and a sedentary lifestyle can all contribute to increased stress levels and burnout. By taking care of their physical health, individuals can better withstand the demands of stressful situations and maintain their resilience in the face of adversity. By prioritizing these strategies, individuals can better cope with the demands of their daily lives and maintain their well-being in the face of stressors. It is important for individuals to take care of themselves and seek help when needed in order to prevent burnout and sustain their mental and physical health in the long term.

3. The connection between self-care and self-discipline

Self-care and self-discipline are two crucial aspects of personal development that are often interconnected. Self-care involves taking care of oneself physically, emotionally, mentally, and spiritually to ensure overall well-being and happiness. It includes activities like exercise, healthy eating, adequate sleep, relaxation, and engaging in hobbies that bring joy and fulfillment. Self-discipline, on the other hand, refers to the ability to control one's impulses, emotions, and desires in order to achieve long-term goals and personal growth. While self-care focuses on nurturing and nourishing oneself, self-discipline is about setting boundaries, making decisions, and sticking to them in order to achieve desired outcomes.

The connection between self-care and self-discipline lies in the fact that they both require a certain level of commitment, dedication, and consistency on the part of the individual. In order to practice self-care effectively, one must be disciplined enough to prioritize their own well-being and make choices that support their physical, emotional, and mental health. This may involve saying no to distractions or commitments that detract from self-care activities, such as skipping workouts or neglecting self-care routines in favor of other responsibilities. Similarly, self-discipline plays a significant role in fostering self-care habits, as it requires a level of commitment and motivation to consistently engage in self-care practices and prioritize one's well-being.

Furthermore, self-care and self-discipline are interconnected in the sense that they both contribute to a positive feedback loop of personal growth and development. When individuals practice self-care regularly, they are better able to manage stress, improve their physical health, boost their mood, and enhance their overall quality of life. This, in turn, can increase their motivation, focus, and productivity, allowing them to achieve their goals and fulfill their potential. On the other hand, self-discipline helps individuals stay on track with their self-care routines and make healthy choices that support their well-being. By exercising self-discipline in areas like diet, exercise, and time management, individuals can establish a strong foundation for self-care practices and create a positive cycle of self-improvement.

One of the key ways in which self-care and self-discipline intersect is in the realm of self-awareness and self-compassion. Self-awareness involves being in tune with one's thoughts, emotions, and behaviors, as well as understanding one's needs, desires, and limitations. By practicing self-care, individuals can cultivate a greater sense of self-awareness and learn to tune into their bodies and minds, noticing when they are feeling stressed, tired, or overwhelmed. This self-awareness can then inform their self-discipline efforts, helping them set boundaries, prioritize self-care, and make choices that support their well-being.

Moreover, self-compassion plays a crucial role in the connection between self-care and self-discipline. Self-compassion involves treating oneself with kindness, understanding, and acceptance, especially in times of difficulty or failure. By practicing self-compassion, individuals can navigate setbacks, challenges, and obstacles with resilience and grace, rather than harsh self-criticism or judgment. This self-compassionate mindset can support self-discipline efforts by encouraging individuals to approach self-improvement with a gentle and forgiving attitude, rather than a punitive or perfectionistic one. In this way, self-compassion acts as a bridge between self-care and self-discipline, nurturing a mindset of self-care and self-acceptance that can support personal growth and well-being. By practicing self-care, individuals can cultivate a deeper sense of self-awareness, self-compassion, and well-being, while self-discipline helps them stay on track with their self-care routines, make healthy choices, and achieve their long-term goals. Together, self-care and

self-discipline create a positive feedback loop of personal growth, resilience, and self-improvement, fostering a balanced and holistic approach to self-development. By prioritizing both self-care and self-discipline in their lives, individuals can cultivate a strong foundation for well-being, happiness, and fulfillment in all areas of their lives.

Chapter 10: Seeking support

1. THE IMPORTANCE OF a strong support system in fostering self-discipline

Self-discipline is a crucial trait that contributes to success in both personal and professional realms. It involves the ability to control one's impulses and emotions and stick to a set of goals or routines, even in the face of obstacles or distractions. However, developing and maintaining self-discipline can be challenging, as it requires consistency, determination, and resilience. In this regard, having a strong support system plays a significant role in fostering self-discipline.

A strong support system consists of people who provide encouragement, motivation, and accountability to help individuals stay on track with their goals. This can include family members, friends, mentors, colleagues, or even online communities. These individuals offer emotional support, practical advice, and constructive feedback that can help individuals navigate challenges and setbacks on their journey towards self-discipline.

One of the key ways in which a support system fosters self-discipline is by providing motivation and encouragement. When faced with the temptation to give up or procrastinate, having a supportive network can remind individuals of their goals and aspirations, and encourage them to keep pushing forward. This constant reinforcement can help individuals stay focused and motivated, even during difficult times.

Furthermore, a support system can also provide accountability, which is essential for maintaining self-discipline. When individuals know that they have someone to answer to, they are more likely to follow through on their commitments and stick to their routines. This external accountability can help

individuals stay disciplined and avoid distractions or temptations that may derail their progress.

In addition to motivation and accountability, a strong support system can also offer practical advice and guidance to help individuals develop effective strategies for building self-discipline. This can include tips on time management, goal setting, stress management, and other skills that are essential for cultivating self-discipline. By leveraging the knowledge and expertise of their support network, individuals can learn new techniques and approaches that can enhance their self-discipline.

Moreover, a support system can provide emotional support, which is crucial for maintaining self-discipline in the face of challenges and setbacks. When individuals experience setbacks or failures, having a supportive network to turn to can provide comfort, encouragement, and reassurance. This emotional support can help individuals cope with stress, disappointment, or uncertainty, and can give them the strength and resilience to persevere in their pursuit of self-discipline. By providing motivation, encouragement, accountability, practical advice, and emotional support, a support network can help individuals stay focused, motivated, and resilient in their pursuit of self-discipline. Therefore, it is important for individuals to cultivate and nurture their support system, and to leverage the power of community and connection in their journey towards self-discipline.

2. Building accountability partnerships and seeking mentorship

Building accountability partnerships and seeking mentorship are crucial components in achieving personal and professional growth. In today's fast-paced and competitive world, having a support system in place can make all the difference in reaching your goals. Accountability partnerships involve partnering with someone who shares similar goals and aspirations as you. This person can hold you accountable for your actions and help keep you on track towards achieving your objectives. On the other hand, seeking mentorship involves finding someone more experienced or knowledgeable in a particular area who can provide guidance, advice, and support as you navigate your personal or professional journey.

One of the key benefits of building accountability partnerships is the added motivation and support that comes from working towards your goals with someone else. When you have someone to share your progress with, you are more likely to stay focused and committed to your objectives. It can also provide a sense of camaraderie and encouragement, knowing that you are not alone in your journey. Accountability partnerships can also help you stay accountable to your actions and decisions, as your partner can offer feedback and hold you to your commitments.

Additionally, accountability partnerships can help you gain new perspectives and insights into your goals and challenges. Your partner may offer a different viewpoint or approach that you may not have considered before, leading to greater clarity and understanding of your objectives. This can be invaluable in helping you overcome obstacles and find creative solutions to any setbacks you may encounter along the way. By working collaboratively with someone else, you can leverage each other's strengths and skills to achieve greater success together.

In contrast, seeking mentorship can provide you with valuable guidance and support from someone who has already walked the path you are currently on. A mentor can offer insights and advice based on their own experiences and help you navigate the challenges and opportunities that come your way. They can also serve as a sounding board for your ideas and help you develop a clear roadmap for achieving your goals. Having a mentor can significantly accelerate your personal and professional growth by providing you with the knowledge and wisdom that comes from years of experience.

Another important benefit of seeking mentorship is the opportunity to learn from someone who has already achieved success in your desired field. By observing their behaviors, decisions, and strategies, you can gain valuable insights into what it takes to succeed. A mentor can also help you avoid common pitfalls and mistakes that they may have experienced in their own journey, saving you time and energy in the long run. Additionally, a mentor can introduce you to new opportunities, networks, and resources that can further support your growth and development.

To build successful accountability partnerships and seek meaningful mentorship, it is important to approach these relationships with a mindset of openness, humility, and respect. Be willing to listen and learn from your partner or mentor, and be receptive to feedback and guidance. Communication is also key in fostering strong partnerships, so be sure to clearly articulate your goals, expectations, and needs. Set regular check-ins and milestones to track your progress and celebrate your successes together. Remember that building accountability partnerships and seeking mentorship is a two-way street, so be prepared to offer your support and guidance in return. By cultivating these relationships with intention and dedication, you can unlock your full potential and achieve greater success in all aspects of your life.

3. Tips for surrounding yourself with positive influences

Surrounding yourself with positive influences is essential for personal growth and development. The people we interact with on a regular basis have a significant impact on our thoughts, feelings, and actions. By surrounding yourself with positive influences, you can enhance your overall well-being and increase your chances of success in various areas of your life. In this article, we will discuss some tips for surrounding yourself with positive influences and creating a supportive environment that fosters growth and positivity.

One of the most important tips for surrounding yourself with positive influences is to be mindful of the people you choose to spend your time with. It is essential to surround yourself with individuals who share your values, beliefs, and goals. By surrounding yourself with like-minded individuals, you can create a supportive network of friends and colleagues who will encourage and motivate you to reach your full potential. Additionally, being selective about the people you choose to surround yourself with can help you avoid negative influences and toxic relationships that can hinder your personal growth and well-being.

Another tip for surrounding yourself with positive influences is to seek out mentors and role models who inspire and motivate you. Mentors and role models can provide valuable guidance, support, and encouragement as you work towards achieving your goals. By surrounding yourself with individuals

who have achieved success in their own lives, you can learn from their experiences and gain valuable insights that can help you navigate challenges and obstacles on your own path to success. Additionally, mentors and role models can serve as a source of inspiration and motivation, helping you stay focused and motivated as you work towards your goals.

In addition to seeking out mentors and role models, it is essential to cultivate positive relationships with friends and family members who support and encourage you. Surrounding yourself with friends and family members who believe in you and your abilities can help boost your self-confidence and provide a sense of emotional support during challenging times. By maintaining strong and healthy relationships with loved ones, you can create a positive and nurturing environment that fosters growth, happiness, and success.

Furthermore, it is essential to be proactive in seeking out positive influences in your daily life. This can include attending networking events, joining professional organizations, or participating in community activities that align with your interests and values. By actively seeking out positive influences, you can expand your network of supportive individuals and create new opportunities for growth and personal development. Additionally, being proactive in seeking out positive influences can help you break out of your comfort zone and expand your horizons, exposing you to new experiences and perspectives that can enrich your life.

Another important tip for surrounding yourself with positive influences is to practice self-care and prioritize your well-being. Taking care of yourself physically, mentally, and emotionally can help you maintain a positive mindset and attract positive influences into your life. This can include engaging in regular exercise, getting enough sleep, practicing mindfulness and relaxation techniques, and setting aside time for activities that bring you joy and fulfillment. By prioritizing your well-being, you can create a strong foundation for personal growth and resilience, making it easier to attract positive influences and cultivate a supportive environment that fosters positivity and success. By being selective about the people you choose to surround yourself with, seeking out mentors and role models, cultivating positive relationships with friends and family members, being proactive in seeking out positive influences, and

practicing self-care and prioritizing your well-being, you can create a supportive environment that fosters growth, happiness, and success. By following these tips, you can enhance your overall well-being and increase your chances of achieving your goals and reaching your full potential. Remember, the people you surround yourself with have the power to shape your thoughts, feelings, and actions, so choose wisely and surround yourself with positivity and support.

Chapter 11: Embracing continuous growth

1. THE MINDSET OF LIFELONG learning and personal development

In today's fast-paced and dynamic world, the importance of adopting a mindset of lifelong learning and personal development cannot be overstated. This mindset involves a commitment to continuously seeking new knowledge, skills, and experiences in order to adapt to changing circumstances, seize opportunities for growth, and pursue personal fulfillment. It is a mindset that encourages individuals to embrace curiosity, resilience, and a growth-oriented outlook on life.

Lifelong learning is not just about acquiring formal education or training, but also about actively seeking out opportunities for self-improvement and personal growth in all aspects of one's life. This could involve reading books, attending workshops or seminars, taking up new hobbies, or engaging in conversations with people from different backgrounds and perspectives. The key is to remain open-minded, curious, and willing to challenge oneself in order to expand one's knowledge and skills.

Personal development, on the other hand, focuses on nurturing one's emotional intelligence, self-awareness, and interpersonal skills in order to become a more well-rounded and self-actualized individual. This could involve working on building healthy relationships, managing stress effectively, setting and achieving personal goals, and developing a sense of purpose and direction in life. Personal development is about taking control of one's own growth and development, rather than relying on external factors or circumstances to dictate one's path.

The mindset of lifelong learning and personal development is essential for success in today's rapidly changing and unpredictable world. As technology advances and industries evolve, the skills and knowledge that were once

considered valuable may become obsolete. Therefore, individuals who are committed to continuous learning and self-improvement are better equipped to adapt to these changes, seize new opportunities, and thrive in their personal and professional lives.

Moreover, cultivating a mindset of lifelong learning and personal development can lead to a more fulfilling and satisfying life. When individuals are constantly seeking to learn, grow, and improve themselves, they are more likely to feel motivated, engaged, and fulfilled in their pursuits. This sense of fulfillment comes from the knowledge that they are actively working towards becoming the best version of themselves and making a positive impact on the world around them. By embracing curiosity, resilience, and a growth-oriented outlook, individuals can continuously improve themselves, adapt to changing circumstances, and find meaning and purpose in their lives. It is never too late to embark on a journey of self-discovery and growth, and by adopting this mindset, individuals can unlock their full potential and create a life that is both rewarding and fulfilling.

2. Setting new challenges and goals for ongoing growth

Setting new challenges and goals is a crucial aspect of ongoing growth and development in both personal and professional spheres. It is essential to constantly challenge oneself in order to continue to learn, grow, and achieve new heights of success. By setting new challenges and goals, individuals and organizations can push themselves out of their comfort zones and strive for continuous improvement.

One key benefit of setting new challenges and goals is that it provides a sense of direction and purpose. When individuals have specific goals to work towards, they are more likely to stay focused and motivated in their efforts. Goals give people something to strive for and help them to stay on track towards achieving their desired outcomes. By setting new challenges, individuals can also expand their skill set and knowledge base, further enhancing their abilities and increasing their potential for success.

In addition, setting new challenges and goals can lead to increased confidence and self-esteem. When individuals push themselves outside of their comfort zones and achieve new milestones, they build a sense of accomplishment and pride in their abilities. This can have a positive impact on overall confidence levels and can help individuals to overcome self-doubt and fear of failure. By setting and achieving new challenges, individuals can prove to themselves that they are capable of overcoming obstacles and achieving their goals.

Moreover, setting new challenges and goals can also foster innovation and creativity. When individuals are faced with new challenges, they are forced to think outside the box and come up with creative solutions to overcome obstacles. This can lead to the development of new ideas, products, and strategies that can drive growth and success in both personal and professional endeavors. By setting new challenges, individuals can continuously strive to improve and innovate, leading to ongoing growth and development.

Furthermore, setting new challenges and goals can help individuals and organizations to stay relevant and competitive in a rapidly evolving world. In today's fast-paced and constantly changing business environment, it is essential to constantly adapt and grow in order to stay ahead of the curve. By setting new challenges and goals, individuals can ensure that they are continuously learning and evolving in response to new developments and trends in their industry. This can help them to remain competitive and position themselves for long-term success. By constantly challenging oneself, individuals can push their limits, expand their skills, and achieve new levels of success. Setting new challenges and goals helps to provide direction and purpose, boost confidence and self-esteem, foster innovation and creativity, and ensure ongoing relevance and competitiveness. It is important for individuals and organizations to embrace new challenges and set ambitious goals in order to continue to learn, grow, and succeed in an ever-changing world.

3. The benefits of constantly pushing boundaries and expanding your comfort zone

In today's fast-paced and competitive world, the ability to constantly push boundaries and expand one's comfort zone is more important than ever. This

is because growth and success often lie outside of our comfort zones, and by pushing ourselves to try new things and take on new challenges, we can unlock our full potential and achieve great things. The benefits of constantly pushing boundaries are numerous and can have a profound impact on both our personal and professional lives.

One of the key benefits of pushing boundaries and expanding our comfort zone is the opportunity for personal growth and development. When we step outside of our comfort zone and try new things, we are forced to confront our fears and limitations and push ourselves to grow and evolve. This can lead to increased self-confidence, resilience, and a greater sense of accomplishment. By challenging ourselves to try new things and take risks, we can develop new skills, build character, and become more resilient in the face of adversity.

Another key benefit of pushing boundaries and expanding our comfort zone is the opportunity for learning and gaining new experiences. When we try new things and step outside of our comfort zone, we are exposed to new ideas, perspectives, and ways of thinking. This can broaden our horizons, stimulate creativity, and inspire innovation. By pushing ourselves to try new things and take on new challenges, we can expand our knowledge and skills, and gain valuable experience that can help us grow and succeed in our personal and professional lives.

In addition to personal growth and development, pushing boundaries and expanding our comfort zone can also lead to increased opportunities for success and achievement. When we step outside of our comfort zone and challenge ourselves to try new things, we can discover new talents and passions that we never knew we had. This can open up new opportunities for growth, advancement, and success in our personal and professional lives. By pushing ourselves to take risks and try new things, we can unlock our full potential and achieve great things that we never thought possible.

Furthermore, pushing boundaries and expanding our comfort zone can also lead to increased confidence and a greater sense of fulfillment. When we challenge ourselves to try new things and take on new challenges, we prove to ourselves that we are capable of overcoming obstacles and achieving our

goals. This can boost our self-esteem, increase our confidence, and give us a sense of accomplishment that can motivate us to continue pushing ourselves to grow and succeed. By stepping outside of our comfort zone and pushing ourselves to try new things, we can build confidence, resilience, and a sense of fulfillment that can help us achieve our full potential and lead a more fulfilling life. By challenging ourselves to try new things, take risks, and step outside of our comfort zone, we can unlock our full potential, achieve great things, and lead a more fulfilling and successful life. So don't be afraid to push boundaries and expand your comfort zone – the rewards are well worth it.

Chapter 12: Practicing gratitude

1. THE IMPACT OF GRATITUDE on mindset and self-discipline

Gratitude is a powerful emotion that can have a significant impact on one's mindset and self-discipline. When we practice gratitude, we cultivate a positive outlook on life and become more appreciative of the blessings and opportunities that come our way. This positive mindset can lead to increased self-discipline, as we are more motivated to work towards our goals and overcome challenges.

Research has shown that gratitude can improve mental health and well-being by reducing stress and anxiety levels. When we focus on the things we are grateful for, we shift our attention away from negative thoughts and emotions, leading to a more balanced and positive outlook on life. This can help us approach tasks and obstacles with a clear and focused mind, making it easier to stay disciplined and motivated in pursuing our goals.

Furthermore, practicing gratitude can enhance our self-discipline by strengthening our sense of purpose and determination. When we are grateful for the opportunities and resources we have, we are more likely to work diligently towards our objectives and stay committed to our personal growth and development. This sense of purpose can help us stay focused on our priorities and make conscious choices that align with our long-term goals.

Moreover, gratitude can also foster a sense of resilience and perseverance in the face of setbacks and challenges. When we practice gratitude, we cultivate a mindset of abundance and positivity, which can help us bounce back from failures and setbacks more easily. By focusing on the things we are grateful for, we can find the strength and motivation to persevere through difficult times and continue working towards our goals with resilience and determination.

In addition, gratitude can improve our relationships and social connections, which can have a positive impact on our mindset and self-discipline. When we express gratitude towards others, we strengthen our bonds with them and create a supportive network of friends, family, and colleagues. This sense of connection and belonging can provide us with emotional support and encouragement, making it easier to stay disciplined and focused on our goals. By cultivating a mindset of gratitude, we can improve our mental health and well-being, enhance our sense of purpose and determination, foster resilience and perseverance, and strengthen our relationships and social connections. Practicing gratitude can help us stay disciplined and focused on our goals, leading to a more fulfilling and successful life.

2. Incorporating gratitude practices into daily routines

Gratitude practices have gained increasing attention in the field of positive psychology and wellness in recent years. The concept of expressing gratitude and focusing on the positive aspects of life has been shown to have numerous benefits for mental and emotional well-being. Incorporating gratitude practices into daily routines can help individuals cultivate a more positive outlook on life, improve relationships with others, and even boost physical health.

One of the most straightforward ways to incorporate gratitude practices into daily routines is by keeping a gratitude journal. This involves taking a few minutes each day to write down things that you are grateful for. This could be anything from something as simple as a beautiful sunrise or a delicious meal, to more significant events like a promotion at work or a loving gesture from a friend. By regularly reflecting on the things that bring you joy and gratitude, you can train your brain to focus on the positive aspects of your life rather than dwelling on negativity or stress.

Another way to incorporate gratitude practices into daily routines is by practicing mindfulness. Mindfulness involves being present in the moment and fully experiencing the sensations and emotions of each moment without judgment. By incorporating gratitude into your mindfulness practice, you can cultivate a deeper appreciation for the present moment and the things that bring you joy. For example, you could practice mindful eating by savoring each

bite of your meal and expressing gratitude for the nourishment it provides. Or you could practice gratitude meditation by focusing on the things you are thankful for and allowing yourself to feel the emotions that arise.

In addition to journaling and mindfulness, there are many other ways to incorporate gratitude practices into daily routines. One simple but powerful exercise is to practice gratitude in relationships by expressing appreciation for the people in your life. This could involve sending a heartfelt thank-you note to a friend or family member, or simply taking the time to verbally express your gratitude for their presence in your life. By focusing on the positive aspects of your relationships and expressing gratitude for the love and support you receive, you can strengthen your connections with others and foster a more positive and uplifting environment.

Incorporating gratitude practices into daily routines can also have physical health benefits. Research has shown that expressing gratitude can lower stress levels, improve immune function, and even reduce symptoms of chronic pain. By cultivating a practice of gratitude in your daily life, you can potentially improve your overall health and well-being. Additionally, practicing gratitude can increase feelings of happiness and contentment, which can have a ripple effect on other areas of your life, such as work performance and personal relationships. By integrating gratitude journaling, mindfulness, and appreciation for relationships into your daily life, you can cultivate a more positive outlook and experience a greater sense of joy and fulfillment. Whether you choose to start small by jotting down a few things you are grateful for each day or embark on a more structured gratitude practice, the benefits of incorporating gratitude into your daily routines are well worth the effort. So why not take a few moments each day to reflect on the things that bring you joy and express gratitude for the blessings in your life. You may be surprised at how much of a positive impact it can have.

3. How gratitude fosters a positive outlook and resilience

Gratitude is a powerful emotion that has been studied extensively by psychologists and researchers for its ability to foster a positive outlook and promote resilience in individuals. When we experience gratitude, we are

acknowledging the good things in our lives and expressing appreciation for them. This simple act of gratitude can have a profound impact on our mental well-being and overall outlook on life.

One of the key ways in which gratitude fosters a positive outlook is by shifting our focus from what we lack to what we have. When we take the time to reflect on the things we are grateful for, we are able to see the abundance in our lives and appreciate the blessings that are often taken for granted. This shift in perspective can help us to cultivate a sense of contentment and satisfaction, even in the face of challenges and obstacles.

Furthermore, gratitude has been shown to have a direct impact on our brain chemistry. When we experience gratitude, our brains release dopamine and serotonin, which are neurotransmitters that are associated with feelings of pleasure and happiness. These chemicals not only make us feel good in the moment, but they also help to rewire our brains over time, making it easier for us to experience positive emotions and outlooks in the future.

In addition to fostering a positive outlook, gratitude also plays a crucial role in building resilience. Resilience is the ability to bounce back from setbacks and challenges, and gratitude can help us to develop this important trait. When we practice gratitude, we are better able to cope with adversity and find meaning in difficult situations. By focusing on the things we are thankful for, we can shift our perspective and find silver linings even in the darkest of times.

Research has shown that individuals who regularly practice gratitude are more likely to have higher levels of resilience and better mental health outcomes. This is because gratitude helps to build a buffer against stress and negative emotions, allowing us to face challenges with a more positive and optimistic mindset. By cultivating a sense of gratitude, we are better equipped to navigate the ups and downs of life and emerge stronger and more resilient in the process.

It is important to note that gratitude is a practice that can be cultivated and developed over time. By incorporating simple habits such as keeping a gratitude journal, practicing mindfulness, and expressing appreciation to others, we can gradually train our brains to focus on the positive aspects of our lives. This

not only helps us to foster a positive outlook and build resilience, but it also enhances our overall well-being and quality of life. By acknowledging and appreciating the good things in our lives, we can cultivate a positive outlook and build resilience in the face of adversity. Through consistent practice and intentional effort, we can harness the power of gratitude to enhance our mental well-being, promote resilience, and ultimately lead more fulfilling and satisfying lives.

Chapter 13: Building confidence

1. STRATEGIES FOR BOOSTING self-confidence and self-belief

Self-confidence and self-belief are essential factors that contribute to an individual's overall well-being and success in life. When a person is confident in themselves and their abilities, they are more likely to take on challenges, pursue their goals, and overcome obstacles. However, many people struggle with low self-confidence and self-belief, which can hold them back from reaching their full potential. Fortunately, there are strategies that can help boost self-confidence and self-belief.

One effective strategy for boosting self-confidence and self-belief is to practice self-affirmations. Self-affirmations are positive statements that reinforce a person's belief in themselves and their abilities. By repeating affirmations such as, "I am capable," "I believe in myself," and "I can achieve my goals," individuals can reprogram their subconscious mind to focus on their strengths and potential. This can help build a more positive self-image and increase self-confidence.

Another strategy for boosting self-confidence and self-belief is to set achievable goals and work towards accomplishing them. When a person sets and achieves goals, it helps to build a sense of accomplishment and reinforces their belief in their abilities. Setting realistic, measurable, and time-bound goals can provide a clear direction and purpose, which can help increase motivation and self-confidence. By breaking down larger goals into smaller, manageable tasks, individuals can build momentum and confidence as they progress towards their goals.

Building self-confidence and self-belief also involves challenging negative self-talk and limiting beliefs. Many people have a tendency to engage in

negative self-talk, such as "I'm not good enough," "I can't do it," or "I'm not worthy. " These self-limiting beliefs can undermine confidence and prevent individuals from taking risks and pursuing their goals. By challenging negative self-talk and replacing it with more positive and empowering thoughts, individuals can shift their mindset and build self-confidence. Counseling and therapy can also be helpful in addressing deep-rooted negative beliefs and building self-confidence.

Additionally, surrounding oneself with supportive and positive people can help boost self-confidence and self-belief. The people we spend time with can have a significant impact on our self-perception and confidence levels. By surrounding oneself with people who believe in and support them, individuals can receive encouragement, feedback, and validation that can help boost their self-confidence. Conversely, toxic relationships or negative influences can undermine self-confidence and self-belief. Building a strong support network of friends, family, mentors, and peers can provide the necessary encouragement and reassurance to help individuals overcome self-doubt and build confidence.

Practicing self-care and self-compassion is also essential for boosting self-confidence and self-belief. Taking care of one's physical, emotional, and mental well-being can help build resilience and confidence. Engaging in activities that bring joy, relaxation, and fulfillment can boost self-esteem and self-worth. Additionally, practicing self-compassion involves treating oneself with kindness, understanding, and forgiveness. By cultivating a positive and nurturing relationship with oneself, individuals can build a strong foundation of self-belief and confidence. By practicing self-affirmations, setting achievable goals, challenging negative self-talk, surrounding oneself with supportive people, and practicing self-care and self-compassion, individuals can boost their self-confidence and belief in themselves. Building self-confidence is a journey that requires patience, perseverance, and self-awareness. By taking proactive steps to build self-confidence and self-belief, individuals can unlock their full potential, pursue their goals, and lead a fulfilling and successful life.

2. Overcoming self-doubt and building a strong sense of self-worth

Self-doubt is a common experience that many individuals face at some point in their lives. It can manifest in various forms, such as questioning one's abilities, feeling insecure about oneself, or fearing failure. However, overcoming self-doubt is crucial for building a strong sense of self-worth and achieving personal growth and success.

One of the first steps in overcoming self-doubt is to recognize and acknowledge its presence. By acknowledging that you are experiencing self-doubt, you can begin to address the root causes and work towards building a more positive self-image. It is important to remember that self-doubt is a normal and common emotion that everyone experiences at some point in their lives. By accepting and normalizing these feelings, you can start to take steps towards overcoming them.

Another important step in overcoming self-doubt is to challenge negative self-talk and beliefs. Often, self-doubt is fueled by negative thoughts and beliefs about oneself. These thoughts can be deeply ingrained and may have been formed as a result of past experiences or negative feedback from others. By challenging these negative beliefs and reframing them in a more positive light, you can begin to build a more supportive and compassionate inner dialogue.

It is also helpful to practice self-compassion and self-care as a way to overcome self-doubt. Self-compassion involves treating oneself with kindness and understanding, rather than harsh criticism. By practicing self-compassion, you can cultivate a more nurturing and supportive relationship with yourself, which can help to counteract feelings of self-doubt. Additionally, engaging in self-care activities, such as exercise, mindfulness, or spending time with loved ones, can help to boost self-esteem and confidence.

Another effective strategy for overcoming self-doubt is to set realistic and achievable goals for yourself. By setting goals that are within your reach and breaking them down into smaller, manageable steps, you can build a sense of accomplishment and success. This can help to boost your confidence and self-esteem, as well as provide you with a sense of direction and purpose. It is important to celebrate your achievements, no matter how small, as this can help to reinforce positive self-beliefs and build a strong sense of self-worth.

In addition to setting goals, it is important to surround yourself with supportive and validating individuals who can help to bolster your self-esteem. Seek out friends, family members, or mentors who believe in you and can offer encouragement and support. By building a strong support network, you can create a positive environment that fosters self-confidence and self-worth. Additionally, consider seeking out professional help or therapy if self-doubt is significantly impacting your daily life and well-being. A therapist can provide you with tools and techniques to help you overcome self-doubt and build a stronger sense of self-worth. By acknowledging and challenging negative beliefs about oneself, practicing self-compassion and self-care, setting realistic goals, and surrounding oneself with a supportive network, individuals can overcome self-doubt and cultivate a more positive self-image. Remember that self-doubt is a normal emotion that everyone experiences, and it is possible to work towards building a strong sense of self-worth through consistent effort and self-reflection.

3. The connection between confidence and self-discipline

Confidence and self-discipline are two essential traits that play a significant role in achieving success in various aspects of life. While they are often viewed as separate concepts, there is a strong connection between them that can greatly impact an individual's ability to reach their goals and fulfill their potential.

Confidence can be described as a belief in oneself and one's abilities. It is the inner strength and assurance that allows individuals to take risks, face challenges, and overcome obstacles. Confidence is often associated with a positive self-image, high self-esteem, and a sense of self-worth. When individuals have confidence in themselves and their abilities, they are more likely to pursue their goals with determination and perseverance.

Self-discipline, on the other hand, refers to the ability to control one's impulses, emotions, and actions in order to achieve long-term goals. It requires individuals to make conscious choices and sacrifices in the present in order to reap rewards in the future. Self-discipline is often associated with traits such as perseverance, self-control, and willpower. When individuals have

self-discipline, they are better able to resist temptations, stay focused on their goals, and maintain consistent effort over time.

The connection between confidence and self-discipline lies in their mutual reinforcement of each other. When individuals have confidence in themselves and their abilities, they are more likely to have the belief that they can achieve their goals. This belief in turn fuels their motivation and determination to take action and work towards their goals. Confidence also helps individuals to overcome setbacks and failures, as they are more likely to view them as learning experiences rather than insurmountable obstacles.

On the other hand, self-discipline is essential for maintaining consistency and staying focused on long-term goals. It requires individuals to resist distractions and temptations that may derail their progress. Self-discipline also helps individuals to stay committed to their goals even when faced with challenges and setbacks. When individuals have self-discipline, they are able to maintain a sense of control over their actions and make choices that align with their long-term goals.

In essence, confidence provides individuals with the belief in their ability to succeed, while self-discipline provides them with the tools to stay focused and committed to their goals. Together, they create a powerful combination that can propel individuals towards success and fulfillment. Individuals who possess both confidence and self-discipline are more likely to set ambitious goals, take risks, and persevere in the face of challenges. They are also more resilient in the face of failures and setbacks, as they have the belief in themselves and the ability to stay focused on their goals. While confidence provides individuals with belief in themselves and their abilities, self-discipline helps them to stay focused and committed to their long-term goals. Individuals who possess both confidence and self-discipline are more likely to achieve their goals, overcome challenges, and fulfill their potential. By cultivating both traits, individuals can unlock their full potential and thrive in all areas of their lives.

Chapter 14: Overcoming obstacles

1. STRATEGIES FOR NAVIGATING challenges and overcoming obstacles

Challenges and obstacles are an inevitable part of both personal and professional life. Whether you are pursuing a career goal, working on a project, or simply trying to navigate everyday life, you will inevitably encounter obstacles that may seem insurmountable at first glance. However, it is important to remember that challenges are not meant to discourage us, but rather to test our determination, problem-solving skills, and resilience. In this article, we will explore various strategies for navigating challenges and overcoming obstacles, so that you can emerge stronger and more successful on the other side.

One of the most important strategies for navigating challenges is to maintain a positive mindset. When faced with a difficult situation, it can be easy to succumb to negative thoughts and emotions, which can cloud your judgement and hinder your ability to come up with effective solutions. Instead, try to approach the challenge with a sense of optimism and confidence. Remind yourself that every obstacle is an opportunity for growth and learning, and that you have the skills and capabilities to overcome it. By maintaining a positive mindset, you will be better equipped to tackle the challenge head-on and find a way to move forward.

Another important strategy for navigating challenges is to break the problem down into smaller, more manageable tasks. When faced with a complex or overwhelming obstacle, it can be easy to feel paralyzed and unsure of where to start. By breaking the problem down into smaller steps, you can create a clear roadmap for how to tackle the challenge. This can help you to stay focused and motivated, as you can see tangible progress with each task you complete.

Additionally, breaking the problem down into smaller tasks can help you to identify any potential obstacles or roadblocks along the way, allowing you to address them proactively and prevent them from derailing your progress.

In addition to maintaining a positive mindset and breaking the problem down into smaller tasks, it is also important to seek support from others when navigating challenges. Trying to tackle a difficult obstacle on your own can be overwhelming and isolating, and it is important to remember that it is okay to ask for help when you need it. Reach out to friends, family members, colleagues, or mentors who may be able to offer guidance, advice, or moral support. Sometimes, simply talking through your challenges with someone else can help you to gain a fresh perspective and come up with new ideas for how to overcome them. Remember that you are not alone in facing challenges, and that there are people in your life who care about your success and are willing to help you through difficult times.

Another effective strategy for navigating challenges is to embrace failure as a learning opportunity. Inevitably, there will be times when your efforts to overcome an obstacle do not succeed, and you may experience setbacks or failures along the way. While failure can be discouraging and disheartening, it is important to remember that it is a natural part of the learning process. Instead of letting failure defeat you, try to view it as an opportunity to learn and grow. Reflect on what went wrong, what you could have done differently, and what lessons you can take away from the experience. By embracing failure as a learning opportunity, you can turn setbacks into stepping stones towards future success.

To recapitulate, it is important to remember that navigating challenges is not a linear process, and there may be setbacks or unexpected obstacles along the way. It is important to stay resilient and adaptable in the face of adversity, and to be willing to adjust your approach as needed. Remember that overcoming challenges is not about achieving perfection, but about making progress and continuing to move forward, even in the face of difficulties. By staying resilient, adaptable, and open-minded, you can navigate challenges with grace and perseverance, and emerge stronger and more successful on the other side. By applying these strategies to the challenges you face, you can overcome obstacles,

achieve your goals, and emerge stronger and more successful on the other side. Remember that challenges are not meant to defeat you, but to test your determination and problem-solving skills, and that with the right mindset and approach, you can conquer any obstacle that comes your way.

2. Cultivating a problem-solving mindset in the face of adversity

Cultivating a problem-solving mindset in the face of adversity is a crucial skill that can help individuals navigate through challenging situations with resilience and effectiveness. Adversity is an inevitable part of life, and how we respond to it can greatly impact our overall well-being and success. By developing a problem-solving mindset, individuals can approach challenges with a sense of optimism and resourcefulness, allowing them to overcome obstacles and grow stronger in the process.

One of the key aspects of cultivating a problem-solving mindset is reframing challenges as opportunities for growth and learning. Instead of viewing adversity as a setback or a failure, individuals with a problem-solving mindset see it as a chance to develop new skills, gain valuable experience, and build resilience. This shift in perspective can help individuals approach challenges with a sense of curiosity and enthusiasm, rather than fear or resignation.

Another important aspect of cultivating a problem-solving mindset is developing a proactive attitude towards problem-solving. Instead of waiting for solutions to come to them or relying on others to solve their problems, individuals with a problem-solving mindset take a proactive approach by actively seeking out solutions, thinking creatively, and taking decisive action. This proactive attitude can help individuals feel empowered and in control of their circumstances, rather than feeling overwhelmed or helpless.

Furthermore, cultivating a problem-solving mindset involves developing strong critical thinking skills. Critical thinking is essential for identifying root causes of problems, evaluating potential solutions, and making informed decisions. Individuals with a problem-solving mindset are able to think critically about their challenges, break them down into manageable parts, and come up with

effective strategies for addressing them. This analytical approach can help individuals navigate through complex problems with clarity and confidence.

Moreover, cultivating a problem-solving mindset involves building strong problem-solving skills. Problem-solving skills include the ability to define problems clearly, generate multiple solutions, evaluate those solutions, and implement the most effective one. Individuals with a problem-solving mindset are adept at applying these skills to a wide range of challenges, from everyday obstacles to more complex problems. By honing their problem-solving skills, individuals can become more efficient and effective problem solvers, capable of overcoming even the most daunting challenges.

In addition, cultivating a problem-solving mindset requires resilience and perseverance in the face of adversity. Resilience is the ability to bounce back from setbacks, adapt to changing circumstances, and keep moving forward in the face of adversity. Individuals with a problem-solving mindset are resilient in the sense that they do not give up easily when faced with challenges. Instead, they persevere through difficulties, learn from their failures, and keep pushing forward until they find a solution. This resilience allows them to weather the storms of adversity with grace and strength.

Furthermore, cultivating a problem-solving mindset involves developing emotional intelligence. Emotional intelligence is the ability to recognize, understand, and manage one's own emotions, as well as the emotions of others. Individuals with a problem-solving mindset are emotionally intelligent in that they are able to stay calm and focused in the face of adversity, communicate effectively with others, and collaborate with different perspectives. This emotional intelligence allows them to navigate through challenging situations with empathy and understanding, fostering positive relationships and effective problem-solving. By reframing challenges as opportunities for growth, developing a proactive attitude, building critical thinking and problem-solving skills, fostering resilience and perseverance, and enhancing emotional intelligence, individuals can cultivate a problem-solving mindset that empowers them to overcome obstacles and thrive in the face of adversity. With a problem-solving mindset, individuals can approach challenges with a sense of

optimism and resourcefulness, leading to greater success and well-being in their personal and professional lives.

3. Building resilience and perseverance in the face of setbacks

Resilience and perseverance are crucial traits to cultivate in order to successfully navigate life's challenges and setbacks. These qualities allow individuals to bounce back from adversity, setbacks, and failures, and continue striving towards their goals. Building resilience and perseverance takes time and effort, but the benefits are immense. It is important to understand that setbacks are a normal part of life and are to be expected. By developing resilience and perseverance, individuals can learn to adapt to and overcome obstacles, instead of letting them derail their progress.

There are several strategies that can help individuals build resilience and perseverance in the face of setbacks. One of the key components is to maintain a positive attitude and mindset. This involves reframing setbacks as learning opportunities, rather than failures. By viewing challenges as opportunities for growth and development, individuals can approach setbacks with a sense of optimism and resilience. It is also important to cultivate a support system of friends, family, and mentors who can provide encouragement and guidance during tough times.

Another important aspect of building resilience and perseverance is developing strong coping skills. This includes learning to manage stress effectively, practicing mindfulness and relaxation techniques, and engaging in self-care activities that promote emotional well-being. By cultivating these coping skills, individuals can better manage their emotions and stay grounded during difficult times. Additionally, setting realistic goals and expectations can help individuals maintain motivation and perseverance in the face of setbacks.

Furthermore, building resilience and perseverance requires a willingness to take risks and step outside of one's comfort zone. This may involve trying new things, taking on challenges that push one's limits, and embracing failure as part of the learning process. By taking risks and pushing past fear and doubt,

individuals can build resilience and develop the perseverance needed to overcome setbacks.

In addition to building resilience and perseverance on an individual level, it is also important to create a supportive and nurturing environment that fosters these qualities. This can be achieved through promoting a culture of empathy, compassion, and teamwork, where individuals feel supported and encouraged to take risks and learn from their mistakes. By creating a positive and inclusive environment, organizations can help employees develop the resilience and perseverance needed to thrive in the face of setbacks. By maintaining a positive attitude, developing strong coping skills, taking risks, and creating a supportive environment, individuals can learn to navigate life's challenges with grace and resilience. Through perseverance and determination, individuals can overcome setbacks and obstacles, and continue moving forward towards their goals.

Chapter 15: Celebrating progress

1. THE IMPORTANCE OF recognizing and celebrating small wins

In today's fast-paced and highly competitive world, it can be easy to overlook the significance of celebrating small wins. However, research has shown that acknowledging and celebrating even the smallest successes can have a multitude of benefits for individuals and organizations alike. By taking the time to recognize and celebrate these small victories, we can boost morale, increase motivation, and ultimately drive greater success in the long run.

One of the key reasons why recognizing and celebrating small wins is so important is that it helps to build momentum and keep individuals engaged and motivated. When we set ambitious goals for ourselves or our teams, it can be easy to become discouraged when progress is slow or when obstacles arise. By celebrating small wins along the way, we can create a sense of progress and accomplishment that can help to sustain motivation and keep individuals focused on their ultimate objectives.

In addition to boosting motivation, celebrating small wins can also have a positive impact on morale and team dynamics. When individuals feel that their efforts are being recognized and appreciated, they are more likely to feel valued and engaged in their work. This, in turn, can lead to greater collaboration, creativity, and a more positive work environment overall. By taking the time to acknowledge and celebrate the contributions of each team member, we can build a strong sense of camaraderie and foster a culture of appreciation and recognition within our organizations.

Furthermore, celebrating small wins can also help to reduce stress and improve overall well-being. In today's high-pressure work environments, it can be easy to become overwhelmed by the constant demands and expectations placed upon

us. By taking the time to celebrate even the smallest successes, we can create moments of joy and positivity that can help to alleviate stress and improve our mental and emotional well-being. This, in turn, can lead to greater job satisfaction, improved productivity, and a higher quality of work overall.

To wrap up, recognizing and celebrating small wins can also have a tangible impact on performance and outcomes. Research has shown that individuals who are able to maintain a positive mindset and focus on their achievements are more likely to persevere in the face of challenges and achieve their goals. By celebrating small wins, we can create a sense of accomplishment and progress that can fuel further success and drive individuals to reach even greater heights in the future. By taking the time to acknowledge and appreciate even the smallest successes, we can boost motivation, improve morale, reduce stress, and ultimately drive greater success and performance. Whether in our personal lives or our professional endeavors, celebrating small wins can be a powerful tool for fostering a positive mindset, building momentum, and achieving our goals. So let us not overlook the significance of these small victories, but instead take the time to recognize and celebrate them with the enthusiasm and gratitude they deserve.

2. Setting milestones and markers to track progress

Setting milestones and markers to track progress is an essential aspect of project management that ensures that goals are met in a timely and efficient manner. By establishing these checkpoints along the way, project managers can monitor the progress of a project, identify any potential obstacles or delays, and make necessary adjustments to keep the project on track. In this way, milestones and markers serve as guideposts that help teams stay focused and motivated towards achieving their objectives.

One of the key benefits of setting milestones and markers is that they provide a clear roadmap for the project team to follow. By breaking down the project into smaller, more manageable tasks, milestones help to create a sense of order and direction, making it easier for team members to understand their roles and responsibilities. Additionally, by establishing specific deadlines for each

milestone, project managers can ensure that tasks are completed in a timely manner, thus keeping the project on schedule.

Moreover, milestones and markers serve as a means of measuring progress and evaluating the success of a project. By comparing actual progress against the established milestones, project managers can assess whether the project is on track or if adjustments need to be made. This enables project teams to identify any potential risks or challenges early on and take corrective action to address them before they escalate into more significant issues.

In addition to providing a roadmap for the project team and enabling progress tracking, milestones and markers also help to keep team members motivated and engaged. By breaking the project down into smaller, more achievable tasks, milestones provide a sense of accomplishment as each milestone is reached, boosting team morale and motivation. This can help to foster a sense of teamwork and collaboration, as team members work together towards a common goal.

When setting milestones and markers, it is important to ensure that they are specific, measurable, attainable, relevant, and time-bound (SMART). This means that each milestone should be clearly defined, with specific criteria for success and a measurable outcome. Additionally, milestones should be realistic and achievable within the given timeframe, and relevant to the overall objectives of the project. By setting SMART milestones, project managers can ensure that they are meaningful and effective in tracking progress and keeping the project on track. By establishing these checkpoints along the way, project managers can monitor progress, identify potential obstacles, and make necessary adjustments to keep the project on track. Milestones and markers provide a clear roadmap for the project team, enable progress tracking and evaluation, and keep team members motivated and engaged. By setting SMART milestones, project managers can ensure that they are effective in guiding the project towards successful completion.

3. How celebrating progress reinforces self-discipline

Self-discipline is a crucial trait that allows individuals to stay focused on their goals and make consistent progress towards them. It involves the ability to control impulses, resist distractions, and persevere through challenges in order to achieve desired outcomes. While self-discipline is often seen as a personal trait that individuals either possess or do not possess, recent research suggests that it can be developed and strengthened through intentional practices and habits. One such practice that has been shown to reinforce self-discipline is celebrating progress.

Celebrating progress involves acknowledging and rewarding oneself for the small victories and milestones achieved along the way towards a larger goal. This can take many forms, from giving oneself a pat on the back to treating oneself to a small indulgence. By taking the time to celebrate progress, individuals are able to boost their motivation, reinforce positive behaviors, and build momentum towards their ultimate objectives.

One of the key ways in which celebrating progress reinforces self-discipline is by creating a sense of accomplishment and satisfaction. When individuals take the time to acknowledge their achievements, no matter how small, they are able to see the progress they have made and feel a sense of pride in their efforts. This positive reinforcement serves to strengthen their belief in their abilities and cultivates a mindset of success, which in turn fuels their motivation to continue working towards their goals.

In addition to boosting motivation, celebrating progress also helps individuals stay focused and on track with their goals. By breaking larger objectives into smaller, more manageable tasks, individuals are able to see their progress more clearly and stay engaged with the process. When they take the time to celebrate each small victory, they are reminded of the progress they have made and the importance of staying disciplined in their efforts. This serves as a powerful reminder of what they are working towards and why it is worth the effort to continue pushing forward.

Furthermore, celebrating progress can help individuals develop a growth mindset, which is essential for building self-discipline. A growth mindset is the belief that one's abilities and intelligence can be developed through effort and

perseverance, rather than being fixed traits. By celebrating progress, individuals are able to see that their hard work and dedication pay off in tangible results, which reinforces their belief in their ability to improve and achieve their goals. This mindset shift can have a profound impact on their self-discipline, as they are more likely to persevere through challenges and setbacks knowing that their efforts will lead to success in the long run.

Another way in which celebrating progress reinforces self-discipline is by creating positive associations with the process of goal-setting and achievement. When individuals take the time to celebrate their progress, they are able to experience the joy and satisfaction that comes from accomplishing their objectives. This positive reinforcement helps to strengthen their commitment to their goals and increases their willingness to put in the effort necessary to reach them. By framing the process of goal-setting and achievement as a rewarding and fulfilling experience, individuals are more likely to stay disciplined and focused on their objectives, even when faced with obstacles and setbacks along the way. By acknowledging and rewarding themselves for their efforts, individuals are able to boost their motivation, stay focused on their goals, develop a growth mindset, and create positive associations with the process of goal-setting and achievement. By incorporating the practice of celebrating progress into their daily routines, individuals can strengthen their self-discipline and increase their chances of reaching their desired outcomes. It is important to remember that self-discipline is a skill that can be developed and improved with practice, and celebrating progress is a valuable tool for cultivating this essential trait.

Chapter 16: Maintaining momentum

1. STRATEGIES FOR STAYING motivated and on track in the long term

Staying motivated and on track in the long term is crucial for achieving long-term goals and creating lasting success. While it can be easy to stay motivated in the short term, maintaining that same level of motivation over an extended period can be challenging. However, with the right strategies and mindset, it is possible to stay on track and continue making progress towards your goals. In this article, we will explore some effective strategies for staying motivated and on track in the long term.

One of the most important strategies for staying motivated and on track in the long term is to set clear, specific, and achievable goals. When you have a clear vision of what you want to achieve and a plan for how to get there, it is easier to stay motivated and focused on your goals. Be sure to break down your long-term goals into smaller, manageable tasks that you can work on each day. This will help you stay on track and make steady progress towards your ultimate objective.

Another important strategy for staying motivated and on track in the long term is to surround yourself with a supportive network of friends, family, and colleagues who can help to keep you accountable and motivated. Having a strong support system can provide you with the encouragement and motivation you need to keep going when things get tough. If possible, find a mentor or coach who can offer guidance and advice as you work towards your long-term goals.

It is also important to maintain a positive attitude and mindset when working towards your long-term goals. Challenges and setbacks are inevitable, but it is essential to view them as opportunities for growth and learning, rather than

obstacles that will derail your progress. Cultivating a growth mindset will help you stay resilient and motivated in the face of adversity, and will allow you to bounce back stronger than ever.

In addition to setting clear goals, building a support system, and maintaining a positive mindset, it is also important to track your progress and celebrate your successes along the way. Keeping track of your accomplishments, no matter how small, can help to keep you motivated and focused on your long-term goals. Take the time to celebrate your achievements and milestones, and use them as fuel to keep pushing forward towards your ultimate objective.

To finish, it is important to take care of yourself and prioritize self-care to stay motivated and on track in the long term. This includes getting enough sleep, eating a balanced diet, exercising regularly, and managing stress effectively. Taking care of your physical and mental well-being will help you to stay energized, focused, and motivated to continue working towards your long-term goals. By implementing these strategies into your daily routine, you can stay motivated and focused on your long-term goals, and ultimately achieve the success you desire. Remember, staying motivated and on track is a journey, not a destination, so be patient with yourself and stay committed to your goals.

2. Overcoming plateaus and preventing burnout

Plateaus and burnout are common challenges that many individuals face in their personal and professional lives. Plateaus are periods of stagnation or lack of progress, where it feels like no matter how much effort is put in, there is little to no improvement or growth. Burnout, on the other hand, is a state of emotional, physical, and mental exhaustion caused by excessive and prolonged stress. These two challenges can be detrimental to individuals' well-being and can hinder their overall success and productivity. Therefore, it is crucial to learn how to overcome plateaus and prevent burnout in order to maintain a healthy and balanced lifestyle.

One of the key strategies for overcoming plateaus is to reassess goals and make adjustments as needed. Sometimes, individuals may find themselves stuck in a rut because they are working towards goals that are no longer relevant or

achievable. By taking the time to reflect on their goals and priorities, individuals can identify areas that may need to be revised or reevaluated. This process of self-reflection can help individuals gain a clearer understanding of what they truly want to achieve and can provide them with the motivation and direction needed to move forward.

Another important aspect of overcoming plateaus is to seek support and guidance from others. Oftentimes, individuals may feel isolated or overwhelmed when they are facing challenges or obstacles. By reaching out to friends, family, colleagues, or mentors for help and advice, individuals can gain new perspectives and insights that can help them overcome their plateaus. Additionally, seeking support from others can provide individuals with a sense of accountability and encouragement, which can be invaluable in times of struggle.

In addition to reassessing goals and seeking support, it is also important for individuals to focus on self-care and well-being in order to overcome plateaus. Taking care of oneself physically, emotionally, and mentally is essential for maintaining resilience and perseverance in the face of challenges. This can involve engaging in activities that bring joy and relaxation, such as exercise, meditation, or hobbies, as well as ensuring proper rest, nutrition, and hydration. By prioritizing self-care and well-being, individuals can recharge their energy and motivation, which can help them break through plateaus and continue to make progress towards their goals.

While overcoming plateaus is crucial for personal growth and development, preventing burnout is equally important for maintaining long-term well-being and success. Burnout can have serious consequences on individuals' physical and mental health, as well as their relationships and productivity. Therefore, it is essential to take proactive steps to prevent burnout before it reaches a critical point.

One effective strategy for preventing burnout is to establish clear boundaries and limits in one's personal and professional life. This involves setting realistic expectations for oneself and learning to say no to excessive demands or obligations. By prioritizing tasks and responsibilities, individuals can avoid

becoming overwhelmed and can allocate their time and energy more effectively. Additionally, establishing boundaries can help individuals maintain a healthy work-life balance, which is crucial for preventing burnout.

Another important aspect of preventing burnout is to practice self-care and stress management techniques on a regular basis. This can involve engaging in activities that promote relaxation and well-being, such as exercise, mindfulness, or creative hobbies. By incorporating self-care practices into daily routines, individuals can reduce stress levels, increase resilience, and improve overall mental and emotional health. This can help individuals cope with the demands and pressures of everyday life, and can prevent burnout from taking hold.

In addition to establishing boundaries and practicing self-care, it is also important for individuals to seek social support and connection in order to prevent burnout. Building strong relationships with friends, family, colleagues, or support groups can provide individuals with a sense of belonging, understanding, and acceptance. This can help individuals feel less isolated and stressed, and can provide them with the emotional support and encouragement needed to navigate life's challenges. By fostering social connections and relationships, individuals can build a strong support network that can help prevent burnout and promote overall well-being. By reassessing goals, seeking support, prioritizing self-care, establishing boundaries, practicing stress management, and fostering social connections, individuals can overcome challenges, maintain resilience, and prevent burnout. By taking proactive steps to care for oneself and seek support from others, individuals can maintain a healthy and balanced lifestyle, and continue to progress towards their goals with confidence and vitality.

3. Techniques for sustaining momentum and consistency

Sustaining momentum and consistency in any endeavor is a critical factor in achieving success. Whether it be in academic pursuits, professional projects, or personal goals, maintaining a steady pace and level of effort is key to making progress and achieving desired outcomes. However, it can often be challenging to stay motivated and on track over an extended period of time. In this essay, we

will explore various techniques and strategies that can help individuals sustain momentum and consistency in their work and endeavors.

One of the first techniques for sustaining momentum and consistency is setting clear and achievable goals. Having a clear vision of what you want to accomplish and breaking it down into smaller, manageable steps can help keep you focused and motivated. By setting specific, measurable, attainable, relevant, and time-bound (SMART) goals, you can create a roadmap for success that will help you stay on track and make steady progress towards your ultimate objective.

Another important technique for sustaining momentum and consistency is creating a structured routine and schedule. Establishing regular habits and routines can help you develop a sense of discipline and consistency in your work. By setting aside specific times each day or week to focus on your tasks and goals, you can create a sense of momentum that will carry you forward even when motivation wanes. Additionally, having a structured schedule can help you prioritize your tasks and ensure that you are making progress consistently over time.

In addition to setting goals and creating a structured routine, it is also essential to stay organized and manage your time effectively. By keeping track of your tasks and deadlines, you can avoid feeling overwhelmed and ensure that you are making progress towards your goals. Utilizing tools such as calendars, to-do lists, and task management apps can help you stay organized and focused on what needs to be done. By staying on top of your commitments and responsibilities, you can maintain a sense of momentum and consistency in your work.

Furthermore, staying motivated and inspired is key to sustaining momentum and consistency. Finding ways to keep yourself engaged and excited about your work can help you overcome challenges and setbacks along the way. One strategy for staying motivated is to celebrate small wins and milestones along the journey towards your goals. By recognizing and rewarding your progress, you can stay motivated and inspired to keep pushing forward. Additionally, surrounding yourself with a supportive community of peers, mentors, and

colleagues can provide you with encouragement and accountability to help you stay on track.

Another technique for sustaining momentum and consistency is to cultivate a growth mindset. Embracing the idea that challenges and setbacks are opportunities for learning and growth can help you maintain a positive attitude and perspective as you work towards your goals. By viewing obstacles as temporary roadblocks rather than insurmountable barriers, you can stay resilient and motivated in the face of adversity. Additionally, seeking out opportunities for feedback and self-improvement can help you continuously refine your skills and approach to your work, ultimately leading to greater success and consistency over time. By implementing these techniques and strategies, you can create a strong foundation for success and maintain a steady pace towards achieving your goals. Remember that progress is not always linear, and setbacks are a natural part of the journey towards success. By staying focused, disciplined, and resilient, you can overcome challenges and obstacles and continue moving forward towards your desired outcomes.

Chapter 17: Harnessing the power of self-discipline

1. THE TRANSFORMATIVE impact of self-discipline on personal growth and success

Self-discipline is a key factor in personal growth and success, as it involves the ability to control one's behaviors and emotions in order to achieve long-term goals. It requires a strong sense of commitment, perseverance, and self-control, as well as the ability to prioritize tasks and manage time effectively. Self-discipline is essential in all aspects of life, whether it be in academics, career, relationships, or personal development. It is a trait that can be cultivated and honed through practice and dedication, and its transformative impact on personal growth and success cannot be understated.

One of the primary ways in which self-discipline contributes to personal growth and success is by fostering a sense of responsibility and accountability. When individuals are able to control their impulses and stay focused on their goals, they are more likely to take ownership of their actions and decisions. This sense of accountability can lead to increased self-confidence and a greater sense of self-worth, as individuals see the direct correlation between their efforts and the outcomes they achieve. In turn, this can inspire individuals to set even higher goals for themselves and push themselves to achieve greater levels of success.

Furthermore, self-discipline can also lead to improved productivity and efficiency. By being able to prioritize tasks and manage time effectively, individuals are able to accomplish more in less time. This can lead to greater levels of success in both personal and professional endeavors, as individuals are able to meet deadlines, take on additional responsibilities, and produce high-quality work consistently. In addition, self-discipline can help individuals

develop good habits and routines that support their goals, such as regular exercise, healthy eating, and consistent sleep patterns. These habits can have a positive impact on overall well-being and can contribute to increased energy levels, improved focus, and enhanced cognitive function.

In addition to its practical benefits, self-discipline also plays a crucial role in personal growth and development. By learning to control their behaviors and emotions, individuals can overcome obstacles and challenges that may arise on their path to success. This ability to persevere in the face of adversity can lead to increased resilience and mental toughness, which are essential qualities for achieving long-term goals and overcoming setbacks. Additionally, self-discipline can help individuals develop a growth mindset, which is the belief that their abilities and intelligence can be developed through hard work and dedication. This mindset can lead to increased motivation, a willingness to take risks, and a greater sense of optimism about the future.

Self-discipline can also have a profound impact on relationships, both personal and professional. Individuals who demonstrate self-discipline are more likely to be reliable, responsible, and trustworthy, which can lead to stronger connections with others. In personal relationships, self-discipline can help individuals communicate effectively, resolve conflicts, and maintain healthy boundaries. In professional relationships, self-discipline can lead to greater respect from colleagues and supervisors, as well as increased opportunities for advancement and leadership roles. Ultimately, self-discipline can help individuals build strong, lasting relationships that support their personal growth and success. By fostering a sense of responsibility and accountability, improving productivity and efficiency, promoting personal growth and development, and enhancing relationships, self-discipline can have a transformative impact on all aspects of life. It is a trait that can be cultivated and honed through practice and dedication, and its benefits are far-reaching. By developing self-discipline, individuals can unlock their full potential, achieve their goals, and lead fulfilling and successful lives.

2. How self-discipline can empower you to unleash your full potential

Self-discipline is a crucial trait that can empower individuals to unleash their full potential and achieve success in all aspects of their lives. It is the ability to control one's impulses, emotions, and behaviors in pursuit of long-term goals and objectives. Self-discipline involves making conscious decisions and taking actions that align with one's values and priorities, even in the face of challenges and temptations. By developing self-discipline, individuals can overcome obstacles, stay focused, and maintain motivation to work towards their goals consistently.

Self-discipline plays a significant role in personal and professional development. It is the key to achieving success in various areas such as education, career, relationships, and overall well-being. People who possess high levels of self-discipline tend to be more organized, productive, and resilient in the face of adversity. They are better equipped to handle stress, set realistic and achievable goals, and stay committed to their pursuits even when faced with distractions or setbacks. By cultivating self-discipline, individuals can build the necessary skills and habits to reach their full potential and create a fulfilling life.

One of the primary benefits of self-discipline is the ability to overcome procrastination and take consistent action towards one's goals. Procrastination is a common problem that can hinder progress and prevent individuals from achieving their full potential. It often stems from a lack of self-discipline and the tendency to prioritize short-term pleasure over long-term success. By developing self-discipline, individuals can overcome procrastination by breaking tasks into manageable steps, setting deadlines, and holding themselves accountable for their actions. This enables them to stay focused, motivated, and productive, leading to improved performance and results in various areas of their lives.

Self-discipline also enables individuals to cultivate positive habits and routines that support their goals and aspirations. Habits are powerful predictors of success, as they shape our daily behaviors and choices. By practicing self-discipline, individuals can create and maintain healthy habits that contribute to their overall well-being and success. This includes habits such as regular exercise, healthy eating, effective time management, and continuous

learning. By consistently following these habits, individuals can boost their productivity, energy levels, and mental clarity, ultimately helping them unleash their full potential in all areas of their lives.

Furthermore, self-discipline allows individuals to develop resilience and perseverance in the face of challenges and obstacles. Life is full of unexpected twists and turns, and setbacks are inevitable on the journey towards success. However, individuals with self-discipline are better equipped to navigate these challenges and bounce back from setbacks with a positive attitude. They have the mental strength and emotional stability to stay focused on their goals, adapt to changing circumstances, and keep moving forward despite adversity. This resilience enables them to overcome obstacles, learn from their experiences, and grow stronger as they work towards unleashing their full potential. By cultivating self-discipline, individuals can overcome procrastination, cultivate positive habits, and develop resilience in the face of challenges. This allows them to stay focused, motivated, and consistent in pursuing their goals and aspirations, ultimately leading to personal and professional growth. By harnessing the power of self-discipline, individuals can unleash their full potential and create a life that is fulfilling, meaningful, and aligned with their values and priorities.

3. Tips for harnessing and maximizing your self-discipline

Self-discipline is a vital attribute that can greatly enhance one's success and productivity in both personal and professional pursuits. It is the ability to control one's impulses, emotions, and behaviors in order to achieve specific goals or objectives. Harnessing and maximizing self-discipline requires commitment, practice, and a deep understanding of one's strengths and weaknesses. In this article, we will explore some tips and strategies that can help you cultivate and strengthen your self-discipline.

One of the first steps in harnessing and maximizing your self-discipline is to set clear and specific goals for yourself. Having a clear vision of what you want to achieve will help you stay focused and motivated, even when faced with challenges or distractions. It is important to break down your goals into smaller, more manageable tasks that you can work on consistently. By setting achievable

milestones for yourself, you can track your progress and stay motivated as you work towards your ultimate objective.

Another key aspect of self-discipline is developing a routine and sticking to it. Establishing a daily or weekly schedule can help you organize your time and prioritize tasks effectively. By creating a routine that includes dedicated time for work, exercise, relaxation, and other important activities, you can avoid procrastination and stay on track towards achieving your goals. Consistency is key when it comes to building self-discipline, so make sure to follow your schedule religiously and hold yourself accountable for completing each task on time.

In addition to setting goals and establishing a routine, it is important to practice self-control and mindfulness in your daily life. Self-discipline requires the ability to resist temptations and distractions that may derail you from your goals. By staying mindful of your thoughts and actions, you can better control your impulses and make conscious decisions that align with your long-term objectives. Mindfulness practices, such as meditation or deep breathing exercises, can help you cultivate self-awareness and improve your ability to stay focused and disciplined in various situations.

Moreover, self-discipline is also about acknowledging your limitations and seeking support when needed. It is unrealistic to expect yourself to be perfect and disciplined in every aspect of your life. Recognize when you need help or guidance, and don't hesitate to reach out to friends, family, or professionals for assistance. Building a support network of people who can provide encouragement, advice, or accountability can strengthen your self-discipline and help you stay motivated during challenging times. Remember, asking for help is a sign of strength, not weakness.

Furthermore, it is essential to practice self-care and prioritize your physical and mental well-being in order to maintain high levels of self-discipline. Taking care of your body through regular exercise, healthy eating, and sufficient rest can improve your energy levels and focus, making it easier for you to stay disciplined and focused on your goals. Similarly, engaging in activities that promote mental wellness, such as mindfulness, journaling, or hobbies that

bring you joy, can help you reduce stress and enhance your self-control. Remember, self-discipline is not just about pushing yourself to the limit; it is also about taking care of yourself and ensuring your overall well-being. By setting clear goals, establishing a routine, practicing mindfulness, seeking support when needed, and prioritizing self-care, you can cultivate a strong sense of self-discipline that will help you achieve your objectives and lead a more fulfilling life. Remember, self-discipline is a skill that can be developed and improved over time, so be patient with yourself and take small steps towards building your self-discipline each day. With persistence and commitment, you can unlock your full potential and accomplish great things in your personal and professional life.

Chapter 18: Conclusion

1. REFLECTING ON YOUR self-discipline journey and growth

Self-discipline is a crucial aspect of personal development and growth. It is the ability to control one's impulses, emotions, and actions in order to achieve specific goals. Reflecting on one's self-discipline journey is a valuable exercise that can provide insight into one's strengths and weaknesses, as well as help identify areas for improvement.

When thinking about your self-discipline journey, it is important to consider where you started and how far you have come. Reflect on times when you struggled to stay on track or stick to a routine, and think about what motivated you to make a change. Did you set specific goals for yourself, or did you simply decide to make a conscious effort to be more disciplined in your daily life. Taking the time to reflect on these questions can help you better understand your journey and the progress you have made.

It is also helpful to consider the strategies and techniques that have been most effective for you in improving your self-discipline. For some people, creating a daily schedule or routine can be helpful in staying organized and focused. Others may find that setting specific goals and deadlines for themselves provides the motivation they need to stay disciplined. Experiment with different approaches to see what works best for you, and be open to adjusting your methods as needed.

As you reflect on your self-discipline journey, it is important to be honest with yourself about your strengths and weaknesses. Acknowledge the areas where you excel in terms of self-discipline, and celebrate your accomplishments. At the same time, be willing to confront the areas where you struggle and consider what steps you can take to improve. Remember that self-discipline is a skill that

can be developed over time, so be patient with yourself as you work towards your goals.

It is also helpful to seek out support and guidance from others who can help you on your self-discipline journey. Whether it is a mentor, coach, or supportive friend, having someone to hold you accountable and provide encouragement can make a big difference in your ability to stay disciplined. Don't be afraid to ask for help when you need it, and be willing to offer support to others who may be on their own self-discipline journey. By taking the time to consider where you started, the progress you have made, and the strategies that have been most effective for you, you can gain valuable insights into your own abilities and limitations. Remember to celebrate your successes, be honest about your challenges, and seek out support when needed. With dedication and perseverance, you can continue to grow and improve your self-discipline skills over time.

2. Embracing self-discipline as a lifelong practice

Self-discipline is a crucial skill that can have a profound impact on our personal and professional lives. It is the ability to control one's impulses, emotions, and behaviors in order to achieve long-term goals. Embracing self-discipline as a lifelong practice requires dedication, persistence, and a willingness to make sacrifices in the short term for the sake of long-term success.

One of the key benefits of practicing self-discipline is increased productivity. When we are able to control our impulses and focus on the task at hand, we are able to work more efficiently and effectively. This can lead to a greater sense of accomplishment and satisfaction in our work, as well as increased opportunities for advancement and success. By embracing self-discipline as a lifelong practice, we can develop the habits and routines that will allow us to consistently perform at our best and achieve our goals.

Another benefit of self-discipline is improved health and well-being. By practicing self-discipline in areas such as diet, exercise, and stress management, we can improve our physical and mental health. For example, by developing the discipline to eat a healthy diet and exercise regularly, we can reduce our risk

of chronic diseases such as heart disease and diabetes. Similarly, by practicing self-discipline in managing stress and taking care of our mental health, we can improve our overall well-being and quality of life.

In addition to productivity and health benefits, self-discipline can also lead to improved relationships and personal growth. By developing the self-control to manage our emotions and behavior in social situations, we can build stronger and more rewarding relationships with others. We can also use self-discipline to challenge ourselves to step out of our comfort zones, take risks, and pursue personal growth opportunities. By embracing self-discipline as a lifelong practice, we can continuously push ourselves to achieve greater levels of success and fulfillment in all areas of our lives.

It is important to recognize that developing self-discipline is not always easy. It requires consistent effort, determination, and a willingness to confront our own weaknesses and shortcomings. However, by approaching self-discipline as a lifelong practice, we can cultivate a growth mindset that allows us to learn from our mistakes and setbacks, and continue to improve over time. By setting realistic goals, breaking them down into smaller steps, and holding ourselves accountable for our actions, we can build the self-discipline needed to achieve our aspirations and fulfill our potential. By developing the ability to control our impulses, focus on our goals, and make the necessary sacrifices for long-term success, we can increase our productivity, improve our health and well-being, enhance our relationships, and achieve personal growth. While the journey to self-discipline may be challenging at times, the rewards of self-mastery and self-improvement are well worth the effort. By committing to a lifelong practice of self-discipline, we can unlock our full potential and create a life of purpose, fulfillment, and success.

3. The power of self-discipline in achieving your goals and living a fulfilling life

Self-discipline is a valuable trait that can greatly impact one's ability to achieve their goals and live a fulfilling life. It is the ability to control one's actions and behavior in order to achieve desired outcomes. Self-discipline is a key component of success, as it allows individuals to stay focused, motivated, and

determined in the pursuit of their goals. Without self-discipline, it can be difficult to stay on track and overcome the inevitable obstacles and challenges that arise along the way.

One of the main benefits of self-discipline is that it helps individuals to stay organized and focused on their goals. By setting clear objectives and creating a plan of action, individuals can use self-discipline to stay on track and avoid distractions that may hinder their progress. Self-discipline also enables individuals to prioritize their time and energy towards activities that will bring them closer to their goals, rather than wasting time on unproductive or frivolous pursuits.

In addition to helping individuals achieve their goals, self-discipline is also essential for personal growth and development. By practicing self-discipline, individuals can cultivate positive habits and behaviors that contribute to their overall well-being and success. For example, individuals who are self-disciplined are more likely to make healthy lifestyle choices, such as eating well, exercising regularly, and getting enough sleep. These habits not only improve physical health but also have a positive impact on mental health and overall happiness.

Self-discipline also plays a crucial role in building resilience and perseverance. In life, there will inevitably be obstacles and setbacks that can derail progress towards goals. However, individuals who possess self-discipline are better equipped to bounce back from adversity and stay committed to their goals. By maintaining a positive attitude and a strong sense of determination, individuals can overcome challenges and continue moving forward towards success.

Another important aspect of self-discipline is its ability to enhance productivity and efficiency. By staying disciplined and focused on tasks at hand, individuals can accomplish more in less time and with greater effectiveness. This can lead to increased efficiency in the workplace, improved performance in academic settings, and better time management in personal endeavors. Ultimately, self-discipline allows individuals to make the most of their time and resources, leading to greater success and fulfillment in all aspects of life. By cultivating self-discipline, individuals can stay focused, motivated, and determined in the pursuit of their goals. Self-discipline enables individuals to

stay organized, prioritize their time and energy towards productive activities, and build resilience in the face of obstacles. Additionally, self-discipline can lead to personal growth and development, enhanced productivity and efficiency, and overall well-being and happiness. By harnessing the power of self-discipline, individuals can unlock their full potential and achieve success in all areas of life.

* 9 7 9 8 2 2 4 9 2 6 1 4 5 *